Dedicated, with respect and admiration, to the more than 600 young men who wore the Silver and Black in league action, the more than 1,000 others who tried to do so, the 12 head coaches and 89 assistant coaches who led them, the many staff personnel who worked with them, the handful of general and limited partners who nurtured them, the 41 million who were present to see them play and the billions who followed them on television and radio these past 39 years. And to those who no longer travel this road, but left glory as their legacy—from 84-year old Ed McGah to 22-year old Leon Bender. For these people—these marvelous people—are truly the GREAT MOMENTS IN RAIDER HISTORY.

THE HISTORY CHANNEL.

THE OFFICIAL NETWORK OF **EVERY** MILLENNIUM

www.HistoryChannel.com

GREAT MOMENTS IN RAIDER HISTORY

Editor in Chief
Al LoCasale

Published by CWC Sports, Inc.

8055 West Manchester Ave., Suite: # 455
Playa del Rey, CA 90293
Tel.: (310) 574-8161, Fax: (310) 448-4299
WWW.CWCSPORTS.com

CWC SPORTS
PUBLISHING & PROMOTION

President Lee Pfeifer

Senior Vice President-
New Business Development
Mark Myden

Vice President-Operations
Louis Coulombe

Publishing Associates
Heckman Media, Inc./Seattle
Jim Heckman President
Craig Olson Vice President

Sherman Media/Chicago
Harry Sherman President

University Publications/Boston
Steve Cadrain President

Sales Associates
John Garms/Detroit, Sam Colton/Chicago, Gulf Atlantic
Industries/Scott Miller/Miami, Tom Myers/Dallas, University
Sports Publications/New York

Vice President National Retail Sales
Steeve Brassard

National Retail Sales
Mike Landman

Vice President Media Services
Ray Raglin

Production Consultant
Patrick Parsons

Administrative Assistant
Sarka Jordankova

SPECIAL THANKS TO:
Champion International Corp.
"The Paper Company"
Greg Burzell   John Hildenbiddle   Kenny Loyd

In searching the four-decade record of the Raiders to select the greatest moments in its proud history, January 15, 1963, must stand out as the single most important date in the organization's history. For on that date, Al Davis was hired as head coach and general manager of professional football's least successful franchise. And from that day forward, the franchise, the league, the game itself was changed forever. A fighter, a pioneer, a brilliant, dedicated football man was now in charge.

A total commitment to excellence has marked the three-time World Champion Raiders monumental rise during the last 35 years to the very top of the professional sports world. During these decades of destiny the Raiders battled their way to the best record in major professional sports.

In these memorable 35 years, the Raiders have had 25 winning seasons, including 16 in a row from 1965 through the 1980 World championship season, and been in the postseason playoffs 18 times.

Davis' four-decade professional football story, from assistant coach of the Chargers, to head coach and general manager of the Raiders, to Commissioner of the American Football League and finally to principal owner and chief executive officer of pro sports' winningest team—the Oakland Raiders—is a standard that no one in the history of professional sports can match for winning and excellence.

In April, 1966, the then 36-year old Davis, head coach and general manager of the Raiders, became Commissioner of the American Football League. This was a post he accepted reluctantly, for first and foremost, Al Davis was a football coach, and knew that assuming the commissionership would in all probability mean an end to his coaching career.

But AFL owners, in their battle with the rival National Football League, prevailed on Davis to accept the position. He was described by AFL president Ralph Wilson as "a coaching genius and astute administrator."

Just eight weeks later, when pro football's two major leagues put an end to their six year war, Davis was acclaimed nationally as the driving force who brought the leagues to merge. In 1969, he was once again a prime force in the dramatic realignment of professional football when two 13-team conferences—the AFC and NFC—were formed for 1970.

As a member of the NFL Management Council's Executive Committee, Davis has been a major factor in achieving collective bargaining agreements with the players. In his extended service on the prestigious Competition Committee he made major contributions to the game and its players.

Al Davis first came to the Raiders in January, 1963, dedicated to rescuing the faltering Oakland franchise and building the finest organization in professional sports. Just 33, Davis was the youngest man in pro football to hold the demanding dual positions of head coach and general manager.

But Davis already possessed 14 years coaching experience. He had been tabbed a "young coaching genius" by *Sports Illustrated* and "the most inventive mind in the country" by *Scholastic Coach* magazine.

In 1963, the Raiders—"picked to finish dead last"—thundered to a 10-4 record and just missed the Western Division Championship. Davis was named Pro Football Coach of the Year.

Perhaps his most singular honor is having made a record eight presentations of inductees to the Pro Football Hall of Fame in Canton, Ohio.

The eight great enshrinees to have selected Al Davis to make the presentation speeches on their behalf are Lance Alworth, Jim Otto, George Blanda, Willie Brown, Gene Upshaw, Fred Bilet-nikoff, Art Shell and Ted Hendricks.

Al Davis himself became enshrined on August 1, 1992 when he was presented for induction into the Hall of Fame by the great former Raider head coach, and now leading television football analyst, John Madden.

But perhaps Al Davis' most lasting achievement has to be his pioneering role in providing opportunities at all levels to members of the minority communities.

In May of 1991, Al Davis was singulary honored as the very first recipient of the NFL Players Association's Retired Players Award of Excellence "for his contributions to the men who played the game."

Born July 4, 1929, Al Davis was raised in Brockton, Massachusetts, and moved at an early age to Brooklyn, New York. He attended Wittenberg College and Syracuse University, earning a degree in English while participating in football, basketball and baseball.

In the late '80s, Al Davis received a Let-terman of Distinction Award from Syracuse University.

In March of 1998, Davis was inducted into the NFL Alumni's "Order of the Leather Helmet," presented annually to "individuals who have made significant contributions to the game of professional football."

In 1950, Davis was named line coach at Adelphi College in New York. He then went into the Army, being assigned as head football coach at Fort Belvoir, Virginia. There he molded a national power service team and capped one season by defeating the University of Maryland, National Collegiate Champions, in a squad game.

Davis next served on the staff of the NFL's Baltimore Colts in 1954, at age 24, concentrating on player personnel work. During 1955-56, he was line coach and chief recruiter at The Citadel. He then spent three years at the University of Southern California as line coach.

In 1960, head coach Sid Gillman hired Davis as offensive end coach of the newly formed Los Angeles Chargers, who won two AFL Division Championships during his three seasons with them. From there it was on to meet the challenges with Raiders of Oakland in 1963.

Al Davis with Buffalo Bills President Ralph Wilson, accepts the position as commissioner of the American Football League in 1966.

Head Coach Al Davis gives sideline advise to quarterback Cotton Davidson in the turn-around 1963 season.

Best Overall Value Winner 1997.
Best Overall Value Winner 1998.

(Best overall reason not to buy a RAV4.)

Standard power windows, locks, mirrors • 16-valve, 130hp DOHC engine • Auto-lock/unlock hubs • Tinted glass • Dual front airbags and driver's knee airbag** • Theft-deterrent system • Driver's adjustable lumbar support • Fully boxed ladder frame • 24-hour roadside assistance • 5-year/60,000-mile drivetrain limited warranty,† 3-year/36,000-mile limited warranty††

THE 1998 KIA SPORTAGE STARTING AT $15,345.*

National Football League
Retired Players

Honor

AL DAVIS

For his recognition of the contribution players have made to the success of pro football.

Al Davis has proved that he cares about players long after they leave the game by:

Hiring former players to football and front office jobs;

Honoring them at Raiders' and public celebrations;

Developing a sense of family among players;

Advising and counseling players as they moved into second careers.

For his many contributions to the men who played the game, Al Davis receives the first

NFLPA Award of Excellence

Presented this 24th Day of May, 1991
at the Seventh Annual NFLPA Retired Players Convention

Jon Gruden—a veteran of seven years of NFL coaching experience and six at the college level—was named head coach of the Oakland Raiders on Thursday, January 22, 1998. Gruden spent the last three seasons as offensive coordinator for the Philadelphia Eagles.

"I like Jon's passion, his resiliency," said Oakland Raiders owner Al Davis. "I've been impressed with him and he got high accolades from everyone that I talked to. I got the feeling that he's got something we need."

One NFL insider labeled Jon Gruden as "a budding superstar, a tough young guy with real old fashioned toughness."

"I'm excited to be here," said Gruden, who as a seven-year NFL assistant saw his teams qualify for the playoffs five times. "I understand the expectations and commitment of this franchise and look forward to getting started. I have vivid memories of the Raiders as a winning team. The Raiders were always in big games. They played physical football. They were prime time."

In 1997, the Philadelphia Eagles ranked second in passing, fifth in rushing and third in total offense in the NFC. In 1996, they led the NFC in passing, were second in rushing and led the conference in total offense. In Gruden's first season as an NFL offensive coordinator in 1995, the Eagles finished fourth in the entire league in rushing.

Gruden, now 35, became the youngest head coach presently employed in the NFL and third-youngest in the 38-year history of

the Silver and Black. Raiders owner Al Davis was 33 when he was named head coach and general manager in 1963, while John Madden was 32 when he was promoted to the head post in 1969.

Before joining Philadelphia, Gruden worked for three seasons with the Green Bay Packers. He served as an offensive assistant to Packers head coach Mike Holmgren in 1992, then spent the 1993 and 1994 seasons as Green Bay's receivers coach. The Packers were 27-21 for those three seasons and were in the playoffs in two of those years. Gruden spent the 1991 football season in the college ranks as wide receivers coach at the University of Pittsburgh under head coach Paul Hackett.

Gruden was an offensive assistant to head coach George Seifert with San Francisco 49ers in 1990, working closely with then-offensive coordinator Mike Holmgren. The 49ers were an NFL-best 14-2 that year, finally losing in the NFC Championship Game.

In his first four seaons in the coaching profession, 1986-1989, Gruden served assistantships at the University of Tennessee in 1986 and 1987 as the Volunteers totaled 17-7-1 and won against Big Ten opponents in the Liberty Bowl and Peach Bowl. In 1988, he was passing game coordinator at Southeast Missouri State and in 1989 coached wide receivers at the

University of Pacific.

Born August 17, 1963 in Sandusky, Ohio, Gruden was a three-year letterman at quarterback at the University of Dayton, graduating in 1985 with a degree in communications. Dayton had a 24-7 record in Gruden's three varsity seasons there. Gruden's father, Jim, is a regional scout for the San Francisco 49ers and formerly served as an assistant coach in the NFL with the Tampa Bay Buccaneers. "I knew I wanted to be a football coach by the time I was 11 years old. My dad would grade films on Sunday morning and I would watch with him."

Gruden's brother, Jay, played in the Arena Football League and currently serves as the youngest head coach in that league with the Orlando Predators.

Gruden and his wife Cindy—a former University of Tennessee cheerleader—have two sons, Jon II, 4, and Michael, 1.

TOP ROW
Frank Gansz, Jr.,Fred Biletnikoff, Willie Brown, Keith Rowen, Chuck Bresnahan, Mike Waufle, Gary Stevens, Dave Adolph

BOTTOM ROW
Garrett Giemont, Skip Peete, John Morton, Willie Shaw, Bill Callahan, David Shaw, Don Martin   (Not pictured–Robert Jenkins)

DAVE ADOLPH, linebackers; born June 6, 1937, Akron, Ohio, lives in Alameda, Calif. Guard-linebacker Akron 1955-58. No pro playing experience. College coach: Akron 1963-64, Connecticut 1965-68, Kentucky 1969-72, Illinois 1973-76, Ohio State 1977-78. Pro coach: Cleveland Browns 1979-84, 1986-88, San Diego Chargers 1985, 1995-96, Los Angeles Raiders 1989-91, Kansas City Chiefs 1992-94, rejoined Raiders in 1997.

FRED BILETNIKOFF, wide receivers; born February 23, 1943, Erie, Pa., lives in Danville, Calif. Wide receiver Florida State 1962-64. Pro wide receiver Oakland Raiders 1965-78, Montreal Alouettes (CFL) 1980. College coach: Palomar (Calif.) J.C. 1983, Diablo Valley (Calif.) J.C. 1984, 1986. Pro coach: Oakland Invaders (USFL) 1985, Calgary Stampeders (CFL) 1987-88, joined Raiders in 1989.

CHUCK BRESNAHAN, defensive backs; born September 8, 1960, Springfield, Mass., lives in Alameda, Calif. Linebacker Navy 1979-82. No pro playing experience. College coach: Navy 1983, 1986, Georgia Tech 1987-91, Maine 1992-93. Pro coach: Cleveland Browns 1994-95, Indianapolis Colts 1996-97, joined Raiders in 1998.

WILLIE BROWN, squad development; born December 2, 1940, Yazoo City, Miss., lives in San Ramon, Calif. Defensive back Grambling 1959-62. Pro defensive back Denver Broncos 1963-66, Oakland Raiders 1967-78. College coach: Long Beach State 1990-91 (head coach 1991). Pro coach: Oakland/Los Angeles Raiders 1979-88, rejoined Raiders in 1995.

BILL CALLAHAN, offensive coordinator and tight ends; born July 31, 1956, Chicago, lives in Danville, Calif. Quarterback Illinois-Benedictine 1975-77. No pro playing experience. College coach: Illinois 1980-86, Northern Arizona 1987-88, Southern Illinois 1989, Wisconsin 1990-94. Pro coach: Philadelphia Eagles 1995-97, joined Raiders in 1998.

FRANK GANSZ, JR., special teams; born August 8, 1962, Greenville, S.C, lives Alameda, Calif. Defensive back The Citadel 1981-84. No pro playing experience. College coach: Kansas 1987, Pittsburgh 1988-89, Army 1990-91, Houston 1993-97. Pro coach: New York-New Jersey Knights (WLAF) 1992, joined Raiders in 1998.

GARRETT GIEMONT, strength and conditioning; born August 31, 1957, Fullerton, Calif., lives in San Francisco, Calif. Attended Fullerton College. No college or pro playing experience. Pro coach: Los Angeles Rams 1990-91, joined Raiders in 1995.

ROBERT JENKINS, offensive assistant; born December 30, 1963, San Francisco, lives in San Ramon, Calif. Tackle UCLA 1984-85. Pro tackle Los Angeles Rams 1986-93, Los Angeles Raiders 1994, Oakland Raiders 1995-96. Pro coach: Joined Raiders in 1997.

DON MARTIN, quality control-defense; born September 17, 1949, Carrollton, Mo., lives in Alameda, Calif. Running back Yale 1968-70. Pro defensive back New England Patriots 1973, Kansas City Chiefs 1975, Tampa Bay Buccaneers 1976. College coach: Yale 1981-96. Pro coach: Joined Raiders in 1998.

JOHN MORTON, offensive assistant; born September 24, 1969, Pontiac, Mich., lives in Castro Valley, Calif. Wide receiver Western Michigan 1991-92, Grand Rapids C.C. 1989-90. Pro wide receiver Los Angeles Raiders 1993-94, Toronto Argonauts (CFL) 1995-96, Frankfurt Galaxy (WLAF) 1997. Pro coach: Joined Raiders in 1998.

SKIP PEETE, running backs, born January 30, 1963, Mesa, Ariz., lives in Alameda, Calif. Wide receiver Arizona 1981-82, Kansas 1984-85. Pro wide receiver New York Jets 1987. College coach: Pittsburgh 1988-92, Michigan State 1993-94, Rutgers 1995, UCLA 1996-97. Pro coach: joined Raiders in 1998.

KEITH ROWEN, offensive line; born September 2, 1952, New York, N.Y., lives in San Ramon, Calif. Offensive tackle Stanford 1972-74. No pro playing experience. College coach: Stanford 1975-76, Long Beach State 1977-78, Arizona 1979-82. Pro coach: Boston/New Orleans Breakers (USFL) 1983-84, Cleveland Browns 1984, Indianapolis Colts 1985-88, New England Patriots 1989, Atlanta Falcons 1990-93, Minnesota Vikings 1994-96, joined Raiders in 1997.

DAVID SHAW, quality control-offense; born July 31, 1972, San Diego, lives in Alameda, Calif. Wide receiver Stanford 1990-94. No pro playing experience. College coach: Western Washington 1995-96. Pro coach: Philadelphia Eagles 1997, joined Raiders in 1998.

WILLIE SHAW, defensive coordinator; born January 11, 1944, Glenmora, La., lives in Union City, Calif. Cornerback New Mexico 1966-68. No pro playing experience. College coach: San Diego C.C. 1970-73, Stanford 1974-76, 1989-91, Long Beach State 1977-78, Oregon 1979, Arizona State 1980-84. Pro coach: Detroit Lions 1985-88, Minnesota Vikings 1992-93, San Diego Chargers 1994, St. Louis Rams 1995-96, New Orleans Saints 1997, joined Raiders in 1998.

GARY STEVENS, quarterbacks; born March 19, 1943, Cleveland, lives in Alameda, Calif. Running back John Carroll 1963-65. No pro playing experience. College coach: Louisville 1971-74, Kent State 1975, West Virginia 1976-79, Miami 1980-88. Pro coach: Miami Dolphins 1989-97, joined Raiders in 1998.

MIKE WAUFLE, defensive line; born June 27, 1954, Hornell, N.Y., lives in Oakland. Defensive lineman Bakersfield J.C. 1975-76, Utah State 1977-78. No pro playing experience. College coach: Alfred 1979, Utah State 1980-84, Fresno State 1985-88, UCLA 1989, Oregon State 1990-91, California 1992-97. Pro coach: Joined Raiders in 1998.

THE GREATNESS OF THE RAIDERS

Professional football in the United States is now in its 79th season. The American Football League came into being in 1960, with the Raiders as the eighth of its eight original franchises. Al Davis took over as head coach and general manager of those Oakland Raiders in 1963—thirty six seasons ago.

Since that January day in 1963 when Al Davis took over the failing Oakland franchise that had won only nine of the 42 league games played by the Raiders, pro football teams have played 7,048 games. The Raiders—in Oakland and Los Angeles—played in 522 of those games, games played at Frank Youell Field, the Oakland-Alameda County Coliseum, the University of California Memorial Stadium in Berkeley and at the Los Angeles Memorial Coliseum.

During those 35 seasons from 1963 thru 1997 the Raiders built a winning percentage of .632—best in professional football and best in major professional sports. There are very few constants in the changing landscape of professional sports. The names change. The athletes and coaches come and go. The uniforms and equipment are modernized. New or renovated stadiums go up throughout the country. Teams now have computerized scouting operations and their own websites.

But among the very rare constants in the game is this continued success of the Raiders. Though the second half of the '90s has been difficult, the Silver and Black continue as professional sports' winningest team.

The Raiders—winners of three World Championships of Professional Football—are the only team to have been in the Super Bowl in the '60s, the '70s and the '80s. Until this past January the Raiders were the only original American Football League team to have won a Super Bowl since 1969—and have already done so three times. In their total domination in these three Super Bowl triumphs, the Raiders outscored the NFC Champions by a combined score of 97-33 for an average victory by over 21 points per Super Bowl. These three big games were history by halftime, as the Raiders

combined leads after the first 30 minutes of play were 51-6.

The Raiders are the only American Football Conference team—and only one of three NFL teams — to have won Super Bowls under more than one head coach.

The Raiders are the only AFC team to have won a Super Bowl in both the '70s and the '80s.

The Raiders are one of only two teams to have gone into the postseason playoffs as a "wild card" team and emerge as World Champions.

In 1993, the Raiders became the first NFL team to have won 300 league games in the four decade span that began in 1960.

For four decades the Raiders have continually defied great odds—both on and off the field—to maintain their unparalleled record. Since 1967, when the Silver and Black won the AFL Championship and went on to the Super Bowl in their very first year in the playoffs, the Raiders have battled their way into the playoffs 18 times, played in 12 Championship Games, won or shared 14 Division Championships in the league's most competitive division, and won the American Football League Championship, three American Football Conference Championships and three World Championships of Professional Football.

Along with owner-leader Al Davis, eight of the greatest players to have worn the famed Silver and Black with pride and distinction, have gone on to be enshrined in the Professional Football Hall of Fame in Canton, Ohio. Five different Raider head coaches, starting with Al Davis in that pivotal year of 1963, have been selected as Pro Football Coach-of-the-Year. Forty-seven different Raider players have been selected for the NFL Pro Bowl and earlier, 29 had been chosen to play in the AFL All-Star Game.

In 1970, as the Raiders began their second decade of play, two exciting new series began in the National Football League. Merged play between the former AFL teams against the NFL teams became a reality. In the 1970-1997 period of interconference competition the Raiders

have compiled a remarkable 66-36-1 mark against NFC opponents.

The other very popular addition to pro football in 1970 was Monday Night Football. The Raiders domination of this prime time ABC Television series has seen the Silver and Black build a remarkable record of 33-16-1 from 1970 thru 1997, including an incredible 12-2-0 record at home.

The Raiders rose from the most humble beginnings. Going 9-33-0 in their first three seasons, the Raiders were floundering—threatening to take the entire new eight-team American Football League down to destruction.

The Oakland Raiders actually played their initial two seasons across the bay in San Francisco—1960 in Kezar Stadium and 1961 in Candlestick Park. Then, in 1962, a 19,000 seat temporary facility was erected on what is now the campus of Laney Junior College in Oakland, adjacent to the Nimitz Freeway, as home of the Raiders.

Tiny, intimate Frank Youell Field became home to a colorful, controversial, crowd-pleasing team that shocked everyone everywhere by winning ten games in 1963—Davis' first year as head coach and general manager. Those ten wins, just one season after the disastrous 1962 season record of 1-13-0, jarred the sports establishment and media alike. In fact, this nine win improvement from one season to the next remains even today—34 years later—as the greatest single-season increase in the first 78 years of play in the National Football League.

An organization of decisive, dedicated, determined people with singular goals was meticulously crafted by Al Davis, who, in 1963, was the youngest man to hold the increasingly demanding role of head coach and general manager. Davis' dreams, nurtured by close personal observation and study of two great baseball organizations during his youth—the New York Yankees, who epitomized size, power and intimidation, and the Brooklyn Dodgers, who represented speed, daring, teaching and the willingness to seek and accept people from cul-

TOP WINNING PROFESSIONAL SPORTS RECORDS 1963-1997

FOOTBALL
OAKLAND RAIDERS
.632

HOCKEY
MONTREAL CANADIENS
.631

BASKETBALL
LOS ANGELES LAKERS
.628

BASEBALL
BALTIMORE ORIOLES
.548

tures not yet accepted in their sport—these dreams became a reality in Oakland.

Frank Youell Field may have been small, a bit shaky and temporary but there was nothing small, shaky or temporary about the football systems and the football organization that Al Davis put together. No, indeed. Frank Youell Field was to become the birthplace of a system of aggressive, attacking, pressure football that revolutionized the game at the pro level.

New, then-unique concepts on offense—the vertical passing game including tight ends and running backs as primary deep receivers, forcing the defense into full-field coverage—were brought into the game. On defense, tight man-to-man coverage utilizing "bump and run" principles, utilization of the three-man front—these Davis devices soon became trends, then became the norm throughout pro football. Innovation, ingenuity, new ideas quickly became Raider trademarks—but so were toughness, tenacity, total preparation and an intense, physical style of play for a full sixty minutes. There was no place to hide when you took the field against the Silver and Black. You tightened your helmet straps for these Raiders for they took no prisoners. They went to war. They came to win!

From "situation substitution" to mini-camps to comfortable training camps away from the Spartan quarters of small college dormitories to things like private postgame parties for players, coaches, staff and their families—the Raiders were ever pioneers, pacesetters, strongly independent, in control of their own destiny, and always imitated, respected and feared.

Football—Oakland Raider football—remains a people game, even in today's high-tech information highway, highly computerized, e-mail filled, website-ready, electronic era. The "O" and "X" are still important, but in the clutch— whether it's on the field or in the office, in the training room, the meeting rooms, the equipment room or, yes—the courtroom—this organization strives to win with great people.

And great people— from top to bottom, headliners or role players— have been as much the Al Davis organizational concept as those simple, uncluttered Silver and Black uniforms worn so proudly by the athletes privileged to play for this very special group.

Thru 1997, 600 players have worn those battle-scarred helmets with the pirate and crossed swords on each side. And all these 600 players are permanently enshrined in the hearts of their teammates and loyal Raider fans everywhere.

Whether one of 11 different men named Smith to have played for the Raiders—Anthony, Bubba, Charles, Hal, James, Jimmy, Jim, Kevin, Ron, Steve or Willie—or the one and only George Blanda, every one of these players made a Commitment to Excellence. Everyone demonstarted Raider Will to Win. The true Greatness of the Raiders has been achieved by players, coaches, staff, administrators, Raiderettes, partners and owner. To them—each and every one—THE GREATNESS OF THE RAIDERS—is a lasting goal, a personal and professional reward, an unforgettable fact of life.

As conqueror of the known world, Alexander the Great once wrote centuries ago—"It is men who endure toil and dare danger that achieve glorious deeds." Such men—and women— have built and maintained THE GREATNESS OF THE RAIDERS.

Your Personal Financial Worksheet

We have the right financing tools to cut your monthly payments in half! Use this worksheet to total your current monthly payment, then give us a call.

Dan Marino, *All-Pro Quarterback*
Spokesperson for FIRSTPLUS Financial

	Outstanding Balance	Monthly Payment
Mortgage Loan	$	$
Car Loan	$	$
Department Store	$	$
Department Store	$	$
Credit Card	$	$
College Tuition	$	$
Personal Loans	$	$
Other Credit	$	$
Your Total Current Monthly Payment	$	

SPECIAL NUMBER FOR NFL FANS **1-888-561-MORE**

RAIDERS VS. ALL OPPONENTS (1960-1997)

Opponent	First Met	Won	Lost	Tied	Winning Percentage
Arizona Cardinals	1973	2	1	0	.667
Atlanta Falcons	1971	6	3	0	.667
Baltimore Ravens	1996	0	1	0	.000
Buffalo Bills	1960	15	14	0	.517
Carolina Panthers	1997	0	1	0	.000
Chicago Bears	1972	5	4	0	.556
Cincinnati Bengals	1968	15	7	0	.682
Cleveland Browns	1970	8	4	0	.667
Dallas Cowboys	1974	3	3	0	.500
Denver Broncos	1960	49	24	2	.671
Detroit Lions	1970	6	2	0	.750
Green Bay Packers	1972	5	2	0	.714
Indianapolis Colts	1971	5	2	0	.714
Jacksonville Jaguars	1996	1	1	0	.500
Kansas City Chiefs	1960	36	37	2	.493
Miami Dolphins	1966	15	6	1	.714
Minnesota Vikings	1973	6	3	0	.667
New England Patriots	1960	13	12	1	.520
New Orleans Saints	1971	4	3	1	.571
New York Giants	1973	5	2	0	.714
New York Jets	1960	16	10	2	.615
Philadelphia Eagles	1971	3	4	0	.429
Pittsburgh Steelers	1970	7	5	0	.583
St. Louis Rams	1972	7	2	0	.778
San Diego Chargers	1960	45	29	2	.608
San Francisco 49ers	1970	5	3	0	.625
Seattle Seahawks	1977	21	19	0	.525
Tampa Bay Buccaneers	1976	3	1	0	.750
Tennessee Oilers	1960	20	14	0	.588
Washington Redskins	1970	6	2	0	.750
		332	221	11	.600

In 1962, third year of play in the young American Football League, the lowly Oakland Raiders struggled hopelessly to be competitive. The effort was there, apparently, but not the leaderhsip nor the talent.

From a fairly respectable 6-10-0 record in the intial 1960 season, the Raiders sank to a dismal 2-12-0 mark in 1961 and an even worse 1-13-0 record in 1962. Their offensive point totals in 1961 and 1962 were the two lowest in the three years of play by the eight AFL teams. And their points given up total in 1962 was the second worst in the fledgling league's history. They gave up 447 more points in their 42 games than they were able to score.

In their 42 league games from '60 thru '62, the Oakland team had won only nine times while losing 33, including 13 in a row in 1963 and 19 in a row from November 11, 1961 through December 9, 1962. They had already gone through three head coaches (Eddie Erdelatz who had a 6-10-0 record; Marty Feldman, 2-15-0; and Red Conkright, 1-8-0) and had used ten different players at the quarterback spot (Cotton Davidson, Hunter Enis, Tom Flores, Chon Gallegos, Don Heinrich, Paul Larson, Nick Papac, Babe Parilli, Billy Reynolds and M.C. Reynolds). They had already played home games in three different stadiums—Kezar Stadium, Candlestick Park and Frank Youell Field. And both Kezar and Candlestick were located in SAN FRANCISCO! Home attendance ranged from a low of 4,821 to a best of 13,000 with only nine of the 21 home crowds exceeding 10,000. For the three year period the Raiders averaged 9,408 fans at their home games. The Raiders were more than inept. They were a disaster that could doom the entire American Football League.

Obviously, things had to change.

And change they did when on January 15, 1963, Oakland Raider president Ed McGah and his partners named Al Davis their head coach and general manager. Davis, then just 33 years old and the youngest person in the modern era to hold these demanding dual jobs, had been an assistant coach on Sid Gillman's very successful San Diego Chargers staff in the AFL's first three seasons. By contrast, the Chargers had been 26-16-0 and had won two Division Championships in those three years during which the Raiders had gone 9-33-0 with two last place and one next-to-the-last place finishes in the same division.

Given complete control of the understaffed and overwhelmed Raider organization, Al Davis immediately attacked the main problem- personnel, on and off the field. A new five-man coaching staff was assembled. Between them, these five assistant coaches would go on to total 44 years of service with the Raiders with four participating in Raider Super Bowl games.

A full-time player personnel department was created with young Ron Wolf, now executive vice

Head coach-General Manager Al Davis instructs running back Clem Daniels in practice.

With plenty of time to look deep, Raider quarterback Tom Flores prepares to go long.

president and general manager of the Super Bowl XXXI Champion Green Bay Packers, in a key role.

But most importantly, quality football players were recruited and signed. A great, experienced wide receiver—Art Powell—was plucked out of free agency to add offensive firepower. Tom Flores, who had missed the 1962 season with illness, and Cotton Davidson were paired at quarterback in a revolutionary new full-field, five man out, vertical passing game. New tight ends and offensive linemen were acquired as Davis worked his national network of contacts to bring in Ken Herock, Bob Mischak, Jan Barrett, Proverb Jacobs, Dick Klein, Frank Youso and Sonny Bishop up front, among others. Center Jim Otto, one of the few high quality holdovers, was given new life and an expanded role, as were running backs Clem Daniels and Alan Miller.

Defensively, tough linemen and linebackers like Dave Costa, Archie Matsos and Clancy Osborne came aboard to put on the new Davis-designed silver and black uniforms. Pass defenders like Claude "Hoot" Gibson, Joe

Krakoski, Jim McMillen and Warren Powers were added as new philosophies of tight coverage and physical play featured the attacking schemes crafted by Al Davis. Gibson as a return man along with Olympic speedster and wide receiver-running back Bo Roberson and kicker Mike Mercer made explosive, big-play special teams a Raider trademark.

The 1963 Oakland Raiders—the name was the same but the game was different. Following the first winning preseason in team history, Al Davis' Raiders topped 30 points in each of their first two league games, winning both. In just two games the 1963 Raiders had topped their winning total of 1962 and equaled their total wins in '61. Then came four close losses in a row. with three during an Eastern road trip. But these Raiders were not the doormats of the early years. No, indeed. These Raiders were not allowed to feel sorry for themselves or find excuses or look for a place to hide.

Al Davis shocked the fans, the football world, the media and everyone else by leading these tough, talented, hungry guys from "Little

Old Oakland" to an eight game winning streak. The games were exciting. The big plays often unbelievable. But one thing was believable. One thing became certain. WILL TO WIN had come to Oakland, California.

The Oakland Raiders finished the 1963 season with a 10-4-0 record, second best record in the entire American Football League, better than every team in the AFC Eastern Division. Unfortunately, however, the playoff format then in use matched the two division champions in the title game and the Raiders were one win short in the tougher AFC West.

But in the nearly 80-year history of the National Football League the Raiders nine-win improvement from the sorry 1-13-0 1962 season to the remarkable 10-4-0 under Al Davis in 1963 is the greatest single season turnaround ever. Ever!

The climb from outhouse to penthouse had begun for the Oakland Raiders. An entire league was saved. The sunny side of the Bay Area now had an identity. Pride had come to Oakland and Alameda County and a new force had emerged forever in professional sports.

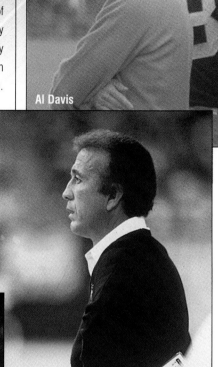

Al Davis

Five memorable moments in the history of the Raiders organization took place when five different head coaches were selected as "Coach of the Year," beginning with Al Davis in 1963.

AL DAVIS	1963
JOHN RAUCH	1967
JOHN MADDEN	1969
TOM FLORES	1982
ART SHELL	1990

In 1963, after the Oakland Raiders had finished with a 1-13-0 record in 1962, worst in all of professional football, Al Davis was named head coach and general manager. An incredible climb to the pinnacle of professional sports was underway. In 1963, Davis led his Raiders to a 10-4-0 record, missing the Western Division Championship by one game. This nine win improvement remains the best single-season gain in pro football history. Davis soon after became the first Raider head coach honored as "Coach of the Year."

In 1967, when Al Davis returned to the Raiders after his dramatic leadership as Commissioner of the American Football League, one of his former assistant coaches—John Rauch—as the new head coach took the club to a 13-1-0 season, the AFL Championship and a berth in Super Bowl II. That single-loss season for the Raiders has been bettered only once in the last 30 years of professional football.

In 1969, Raider managing general partner Al Davis again reached into the team's coaching staff to name 33-year-old John Madden as head coach of the Silver and Black. The intense, affable Madden readily accepted the challenge and took the Raiders to a 12-1-1 league campaign and an eventual

spot in the Conference Championship Game. Madden went onto become the youngest head coach in the modern pro football era to win 100 games in his first ten seasons.

In 1982, amidst the turbulent uncertainty of the franchise relocation and the 55-day mid-season player's strike, Tom Flores calmly directed the Raiders to an 8-1-0 record, best in the league in that strike-shortened season. Flores, another former Raider assistant as well as the team's original quarterback back in the start-up season of 1960, put the team back in the playoffs for the 12th time in a 16-year span. Flores' Raiders won a Super Bowl after the 1980 and 1983 seasons.

Then, in 1990, in just his first full season as head coach of the Los Angeles Raiders, Art Shell directed the team to an impressive 12-4-0 record and to the playoffs for the 16th

John Madden

Tom Flores

Art Shell

time. The former All Pro Raider offensive tackle—a future Pro Football Hall of Fame member—had been an assistant coach with the organization after 15 seasons in the offensive line. Shell joined Al Davis and John Madden as Raider head coaches named Coach of the Year in their very first season on the job. ◆

John Rauch

This is not an Independent Insurance Agent...

...It's your most important Business Partner

In today's complex world of insurance, you need a proven professional who can help you compete. Your Independent Insurance Agent knows the insurance needs of your business, and your community. Put them to work for you and take advantage of their years of experience. If you do, you'll realize what we at Travelers have known for over 130 years. The Independent Insurance Agent is your most valuable business partner.

We've made choosing the right business partner easier.
Call your local Travelers Agent today.

X E R O X

of the san francisco bay

It's not just a letter. It's a way to get work done.

The letter is X. The company is Xerox. And the story is all about change.

Change is something we're comfortable with at Xerox. It's what we've been doing since the day we created the first copier, and changed forever the way people work with documents.

Indeed, we've built our business by following the document wherever it takes us. Today, few things in business change as fast as the document. It begins on a computer screen. It moves around the world on interactive, electronic networks. It exists in multimedia environments. It can be scanned, stored, retrieved, revised, distributed, printed and published where, when and how you want it.

In short, the document is constantly moving from digital form to paper, and back again. Which is why now, more than ever, our mission as The Document Company is clear: to put together the innovative document services

you need—the systems, solutions, products and people— to make your business more productive.

It is also why this new "digitized" X is more than a letter to us. It is a symbol of change and vitality in the newly emerging digital world. It represents everything we do to help you get your work done, and make your life at work a little more satisfying and rewarding.

We'll be using this new symbol in many different ways, so keep your eyes open for it.

For us, it signals the next step in a long Xerox tradition of taking the first step into the future. And in a world that won't stop changing, that's still the most productive step anyone can take.

THE
DOCUMENT
COMPANY
XEROX
Worldwide Sponsor

THE DOCUMENT COMPANY
XEROX

Xerox of the San Francisco Bay

201 Spear Street • San Francisco, CA 94105 • (415) 227-1700

475 Fourteenth Street • Oakland, CA 94612 • (510) 433-3200

CONQUEST

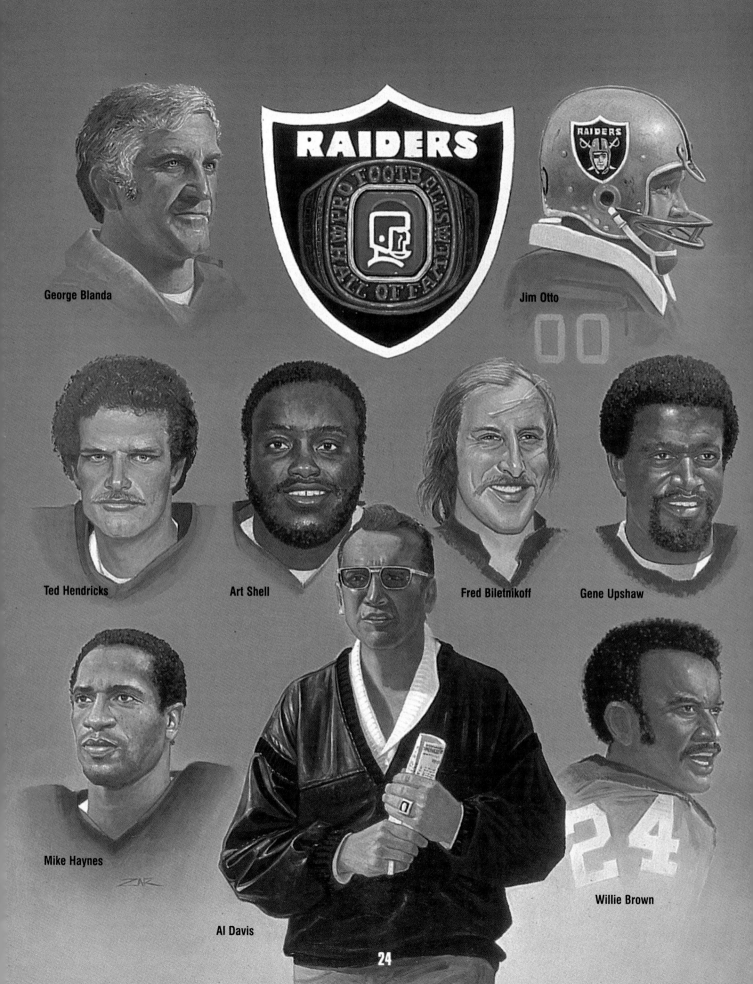

George Blanda

Jim Otto

Ted Hendricks

Art Shell

Fred Biletnikoff

Gene Upshaw

Mike Haynes

Al Davis

Willie Brown

24

The Pro Football Hall of Fame is located in Canton, Ohio, approximately 53 miles south of Cleveland, 100 miles west of Pittsburgh and within 225 miles of such pro football centers as Buffalo,

ENSHRINEMENT, that is the word used when one becomes a Pro Football Hall of Famer. For this is the shrine, the single center for recognition as one of the lasting, all-time greats of the game.

before the Super Bowl. The only limitation on selection is that a player must have been retired at least five years and a coach must be retired. Other contributors (owners, administrative personnel, etc.) may be

RAIDERS IN THE PRO FOOTBALL HALL OF FAME

Name	Position	Date Enshrined
JIM OTTO	Center	August 2, 1980
GEORGE BLANDA	Quarterback-Kicker	August 1, 1981
WILLIE BROWN	Cornerback	July 28, 1984
GENE UPSHAW	Guard	August 8, 1987
FRED BILETNIKOFF	Wide Receiver	July 30, 1988
ART SHELL	Offensive Tackle	August 5, 1989
TED HENDRICKS	Linebacker	August 4, 1990
AL DAVIS	Coach, Owner, Commissioner, Team Administrator	August 1, 1992
MIKE HAYNES	Cornerback	July 26, 1997

Cincinnati and Detroit.

However, wherever this collection of buildings, exhibits, memorabilia and the like, is located, it is never far from the hearts of those who play the game. Membership in the Pro Football Hall of Fame is the epitome of individual achievement for players, coaches and administrators who have given much of their love and much of their lives to professional football. In fact, membership is not the term used to designate the less than 200 people now in the Hall of Fame.

Election of new members to the Hall of Fame is solely the responsibility of a Board of Selectors, largely made up of sports writers. Each pro football city is represented. The Board meets each year on the day

nominated and elected while they are still active.

Presently, there are nine great Raiders enshrined in the Professional Football Hall of Fame.

"Commitment to Excellence, Pride and Poise, the Greatness of the Raiders, were not only exemplified by Jim Otto - they were Jim Otto."

Those were the words of Raider owner Al Davis following Jim Otto's selection to the Pro Football Hall of Fame in 1980. Indeed, for 15 memorable seasons the legendary center created a standard of excellence to be followed by all future Raiders for four glorious decades.

Statistics in part illustrate the conviction Jim Otto had for individual and team pride. He never missed a regular season game during his pro career, posting 210 consecutive games—every one as a starter. When you include preseason, postseason and All-Star game appearances, Otto played in an amazing total of 308 games.

For 13 consecutive seasons Jim Otto was an All-Pro. During its 10-year history, the American Football League never had another All-League center. And for the first three years of play following the AFL-NFL merger, Otto was the All-AFC choice at center.

Team success coincided with Jim Otto's individual achievements. In his final eight seasons, Otto led the Raiders to seven division championships and the AFL crown in 1967.

But it was during his earlier years that Otto made his most significant contributions. In fact, the 6-2, 250 pound lineman was often the lone shining star for a team that struggled badly.

When Jim Otto first came to the Raiders in 1960, the franchise was floundering so badly it didn't even have a permanent practice field. The team's chances seemed remote, at best. It seemed very unlikely that an undersized rookie center from the University of Miami could improve the chaotic situation.

Yet, in spite of sometimes marginal talent around him, Otto emerged as the AFL's premier center from the league's very outset. Considered too small by NFL minimums, he was passed over in the older league's draft and not even offered a free agent contract. Otto was, however, selected in the 25th round of the first AFL draft by the Minneapolis franchise, which soon transferred to Oakland.

A two-way performer in college, Otto decided that his best chance to make the Raiders would be at center.

"I knew I'd have to play offense," he recalls. "Even though I really liked defense, I got hurt too often there. When I came to the Raiders head coach Eddie Erdelatz was trying everybody on both sides of the ball and wanted to use me at linebacker. I'd take it easy on defense and really get after it on offense and somehow I

looked better than anybody else on offense. So, I stayed there."

In those early years, the Raiders were little more than a joke—a bad joke. In 1961-1962, the team lost an AFL record 19 games in a row.

The Raiders 9-33-0 record from 1960 thru 1962 was no surprise to Otto. "We just didn't have many good players. The club was unable to sign its draft picks. They'd bring people into camp but that's all they were—people. They certainly weren't players."

That quickly changed when Al Davis arrived as head coach and general manager in 1963. Acquiring real talent and installing a wide-open offense and an attacking defense, Davis turned the club from a sorry 1-13-0 in '62 to a soaring 10-4-0 in '63. For Otto, that 1963 season was a real learning experience.

"Coach Davis brought in a different system—something people weren't expecting from us," explains Otto. "That first year I

thought I'd never learn it. I'd dream about it at night and wake up shouting signals. Then I'd know I had the signals wrong and have to get out my playbook and get things right."

Eventually, Otto and his teammates learned the new system and began to build a winner. By 1967, the AFL Championship belonged to the proud wearers of the Silver and Black.

"Those early years were tough," remembers Otto. "But Al Davis came in, took over the situation, recognized it, reorganized it, and made the Raiders into the dynamic organization that dominated recent decades. When he came in I could see the light at the end of the tunnel.

Jim Otto remained an inspiration to fellow Raiders throughout his long career, with a never-satisfied desire to be the very best.

Willie Brown, the Raiders brilliant cornerback, who joined Otto in the Hall of Fame in 1984, recalls his playing days with the inspirational center. "When I first joined the Raiders, I discovered right away that Jim had a lot of pride in himself. I learned how to be more dedicated toward my position because of his outlook. He taught me a lot about individual and team pride. I don't think there can be the Raiders without Jim Otto."

No biography of Jim Otto would be complete without mentioning his legendary jersey number- 00—"Double 0."

"Some people claim I would never have made All-League if I had another number," says Otto. "But I made it my first year and I was wearing 50 then. Double-0 made it more noticeable when I did something right, but it also made it more noticeable if I did something wrong."

Jim Otto loved the game of football and even more he loved the Raiders. As special projects director for the organization, he still attends every Raider game, home or away. "Once a Raider, always a Raider," started with Jim Otto.

Perhaps the most accurate description of "Double-0" as a player was offered by his former coach, the great John Madden:

"Remember those movies in which a guy walks in with his football shoes draped over his shoulder, rubs dirt in his palm and says, 'Let's go', well, that's Jim Otto."

When you're 39 years old and a veteran of 17 seasons of pro football, you shouldn't have much left to prove. But George Blanda felt he still had much to prove when he joined the Oakland Raiders in 1967.

His previous AFL team—the Houston Oilers—had just "retired" the quarterback-kicker, claiming little use for a player his age. Blanda thought he could still do the job if only someone would give him the chance.

"Then," Blanda recalls, "Al Davis calls and tells me I belong to them."

Blanda responded by giving the Raiders nine years of unforgetable football. He also became a folk hero across America.

George Blanda originally entered pro football in 1949 as a 12th round draft choice of the Chicago Bears, after playing his college ball at Kentucky. During his 10 seasons with Chicago, Blanda moved in and out of the starting quarterback job while doing most of the place kicking as well.

His association with the Bears ended in 1958 when George Halas labeled Blanda as "too old." Blanda quit, sat out the 1959 season and signed on with the Houston Oilers of the newly-formed American Football League in 1960.

The birth of the AFL gave George Blanda a second football life, and he responded by leading the Oilers to the championship in their first two seasons. Both championship victories came over Chargers teams on which Al Davis was a coach. Those games would stay alive in Davis' memory.

In 1961, Blanda set a pro football record with 36 touchdown passes in a 14-game season, but his accomplishments were mostly ignored as pro-NFL media proclaimed the AFL as a minor league. Blanda still resents that.

"I think the AFL might have won the Super Bowl as early as 1960 or 1961," he states with conviction. "We had a fine team, and the NFL will never be able to prove that we couldn't have beaten them."

Blanda remained the Oilers top quarterback thru 1966, though the Oilers were not nearly as successful as earlier and fickle Houston fans began to boo for his escalating interception totals.

"When you're down by 14 points, I'd rather be throwing and trying to win than play it safe and lose by 14," reasons Blanda. "I'd rather throw 300 interceptions in my career than never win a championship."

This highly-competitive nature helped earn Blanda a place on the Raider roster. Blanda was an important factor as the Raiders won their first AFL Championship in 1967, as he led the

league in scoring with 116 points in the 14 game season and served effectively as a back-up quarterback to Daryle Lamonica. In a similar role in 1969 Blanda scored 117 points.

In 1970, Blanda was placed on waivers during the preseason and considered retirement. But Al Davis assured him that the waiver move was a tactical one to protect a young quarterback by the name of Ken Stabler and that Blanda would again be on the active squad when the season opened. Blanda stayed and began a season that was later described by Raider Radio voice Bill King as "one part fantasy, one part imagination and one part miracle."

On October 25, 1970, against the Steelers, Blanda came off the bench to replace injured Daryle Lamonica, threw for three touchdowns and kicked a field goal to lead the Raiders to a 31 -14 victory.

Next, in Kansas City, he kicked a 48-yard field goal with just three seconds remaining to earn a tie against the Chiefs, 17-17.

The following Sunday, Blanda again stepped in for Lamonica to throw a touchdown to tie Cleveland at 20 all with 1:34 remaining, and then kick a 52-yard field goal with three seconds left to beat the Browns, 23-20.

The magic continued the next week when Blanda threw a touchdown pass with 2:28 left to defeat the Denver Broncos, 24-19.

He completed his five-game miracle streak with a 16-yard field goal with seven seconds left to down San Diego, 20-17.

George Blanda pulled off other miracles and near-miracles that season and at the age of 43 became the oldest quarterback to play in a Championship Game. Although the Raiders lost to the Colts. Blanda accounted for all 17 points for the Silver and Black.

For his great efforts and accomplishments, Blanda was honored as the AFC Player of the Year for 1970 as well as the NFL Man of the Year for his deeds both on and off the field.

The Youngblood, Pennsylvania native played five more years for the Raiders before retiring prior to the 1976 season, just weeks before his 49th birthday. He had scored 2,002 points and played in 340 league games—records that remain unchallenged even now.

"When I look back on my nine years with the Raiders, what comes to mind first is my great association with Al Davis," says Blanda. "If it had not been for him I may not have done the things I did after leaving the Oilers. I may not even have kept playing if it weren't for him."

"It was great to be a part of a winning organization with some of the best coaches, greatest players, the Pride and Poise…everything."

Al Davis has equal praise for George Blanda, who was elected to the Pro Football Hall of Fame in 1981.

"He's the greatest competitor the game has ever seen. Some may have been his equal, but none greater. Pride and Poise, Commitment to Excellence, go hand in hand with George Blanda," says Davis.

30

Professional football has been blessed by the exploits of many great players now enshrined in the Pro Football Hall of Fame. Only a very select few, however, can truly claim to have revolutionized the game thru their style of play. One such rare player was Willie Brown, the superlative Raider cornerback who put "bump-and-run" in the football vocabulary.

Willie Brown's aggressive, face mask to face mask style changed the concepts of pass defense in pro football. He was the first cornerback to pick up a receiver right at the line of scrimmage, jolting or bumping him off his stride, directing his release to alter his timing and his route.

"The great thing about it is that it confuses the receiver," says Brown. "Anything that breaks up the timing of the quarterback is good. Plus, you don't always have to bump-and-run. A majority of the time I never even hit anybody, but the reputation and the threat of this thing got around."

Brown built his reputation with outstanding play for 16 seasons. In each of those seasons he had at least one pass interception—an NFL record. All told, Brown intercepted 54 passes, including 39 during 12 seasons in Silver and Black for a club record now shared by Lester Hayes.

A graduate of Grambling, Brown was originally signed as a free agent by the Houston Oilers in 1963, after being passed up in the college draft by the AFL and the NFL. Houston cut him before the '63 season began and he then signed with the Denver Broncos.

Brown quickly established himself as a great player in Denver. In his second season there, the 6-2, 215 pounder intercepted a career-high nine passes, including a record-tying four in a game against the New York Jets. Brown capped the year with an MVP performance in the AFL All-Star Game.

Before the start of the 1967 season, Brown was traded to the Oakland Raiders. That first season in Silver and Black he picked off seven passes, helping the Raiders to their first AFL Championship and to Super Bowl II, as well as earning himself a spot on the All-League team.

As Willie Brown's reputation as a pass defender grew, opposing quarterbacks began to stay away from his side. Some of his peers even referred to him as the "lonesome cornerback."

"I felt that if I covered my man and forced the play elsewhere, I was doing my job," recalls Brown. "But I was never lonely, not with all those people in the stands and on the sidelines looking at me. There was no time to relax. Besides, it's instinctive for a cornerback to think every play is coming his way."

For Brown, those instincts were sharpened in daily in which he maintained the same level of intensity he had on game day.

"You have to play each down in practice as if it were in a game in order to accomplish what you need to. You have to work in practice in order to prepare to be ready," Brown explains. "In order to accomplish what you want to, there's no way you can go half-speed during the week and then try to get it together on Sunday."

A seven-time All-League selection, Brown played in five AFL All-Star Games and four AFC-NFC Pro Bowls. Individual accolades aside, however, Brown always seemed to play his best during the Playoffs. His three career-postseson touchdowns on interception returns is an NFL record. His most memorable scoring steal occurred during Super Bowl XI against that year's NFC best—the Minnesota Vikings.

Former Kansas City head coach Hank Stram, who faced Willie Brown twice a year in Chiefs-Raiders duels, once observed, "You don't dare the out to Brown's side," but veteran Viking QB Fran Tarkenton decided to do just that midway thru the fourth quarter.

"I noticed the Vikings lined up without a huddle so I figured Tarkenton was going to an 'out' pattern," Brown recalls. "When he took two steps back, it was the tip-off. I played that out all the way."

Brown's 75-yard touchdown set a Super Bowl record. It also concluded the scoring for the Raiders as they completely dominated the Vikings, 32-14.

"Winning the Super Bowl meant 14 years of hard work paid off by accomplishing goals that I had set when I first started playing football," says Brown. "Winning the Super Bowl is the number one goal of every player. He wants to win it sometime during his career."

Brown retired as a player before the 1979 season and then served as a Raider assistant coach. He added two more Super Bowl rings to his collection in that capacity as the Raiders conquered the Philadelphia Eagles, 27-10, in Super Bowl XV in the Louisiana Superdome and the Washington Redskins, 38-9, in Super Bowl XVIII in Tampa. The win over the Redskins had special meaning for Willie Brown personally and professionally. For in that game, two of his outstanding pupils—Lester Hayes and future Hall of Famer Mike Haynes—performed brilliantly using bump-and-run principles, blanketing the Washington wide receivers.

On the day Willie Brown was inducted into the Pro Football Hall of Fame—July 28, 1984—his presenter, Al Davis, referred to that superb play by Hayes and Haynes in Super Bowl XVIII.

"Willie Brown was their coach," Davis pointed out. "Willie Brown was their inspiration. It was a reaffirmation of his style of play that began with the Raiders in the sixties."

Davis concluded that enshrinement speech by saying, "Willie Brown will be the standard of excellence by which cornerbacks are judged in the years to come. But time cannot defeat him, for the legend of Willie Brown will live on in Camelot—the Pro Football Hall of Fame."

In 1967, Raider Managing General Partner Al Davis, in planning to overtake the powerful Kansas City Chiefs to finish atop the tough AFL Western Division, sought a special type of athlete in the coming college player draft—someone with the size, speed, strength, talent and temperment to handle great defensive tackles like Buck Buchanan of the Chiefs. Matchups—an Al Davis football philosophy—mandated that Oakland not allow an opponent to be able to dominate at key spots. Accordingly, a great guard was needed—and needed now.

Many pro scouts would not agree—they rarely do where Raider draft picks are concerned—but the Oakland staff felt that exactly what they needed was available deep in the heart of Texas. In Kleeburg County in the southeast corner of that state—famed as the home of the huge King Ranch—lay Kingsville, Texas and Texas A&I University. There Gil Steinke, a former hard-nosed defensive back with the Philadelphia Eagles, had developed a tough, winning football operation, just 125 miles north of the Rio Grande.

This was cattle country, cotton country and U.S. Navy country, with nearby Corpus Christi and Kingsville Naval Air Stations. But just about anywhere in Texas was also football country.

In the offensive line at Texas A&I was a tall, trim, agile, active blocker named Eugene Upshaw. Gene did not look like he carried 250 pounds on his six-foot, five-inch frame, particularly when you watched him move. For Gene had fullback speed—4.8 seconds or less for 40 yards. He could pull and lead the sweeps, block inside and pass protect against the big guys. He had quick feet and a mind to match.

There were rough edges, of course, but the talent was obvious. As the Raiders 1967 first-round draft choice, Upshaw got notoriety, a sizeable contract and quickly moved in at the starting left guard position. Oakland offensive line coach Ollie Spencer knew the organization had found a great player to go to the left of

perennial All-AFL center Jim Otto—and it stayed that way for the next 15 years!

As Upshaw recalls, "This was a great way to start your pro football career. You get picked in the first round, sign your name about a dozen times on the contract. They hand you a nice check, give you a black jersey, put you in the starting lineup and six months later you're playing in the Super Bowl."

The Raiders lost that Super Bowl to the

Green Bay Packers in the Orange Bowl in Miami. It would be the only Super Bowl loss for the Silver and Black in four such World Championship Games. That single loss ate at Gene Upshaw's insides. He never forgot it and the smug air of superiority exhibited by those 1967 NFL Champions and their cohorts in the media.

Nine years—and 103 victories—later, the Raiders returned to the Super Bowl. This time they represented the American Football Conference. This time the game—Super Bowl XI—was to be played in the mammoth Rose Bowl in Pasadena, California. This time Gene Upshaw was offensive captain of the Oakland Raiders who were going into the World Championship contest with a record of 15-1-0 so far in 1976 and a team that had five future

Pro Football Hall of Fame enshrinees on its playing roster plus one in the owner's box. And now when Upshaw spoke, everyone listened. He was no longer a highly-touted but unproven rookie. No, indeed! He had already been selected for the Pro Bowl five times.

At the squad meeting the week before the Super Bowl game, Captain Upshaw told his teammates "There isn't any reason to go to the Super Bowl if you're not going to win it. Nobody remembers who loses Super Bowls, just who wins. Forget your relatives who need tickets and your wife who wants shopping trips and the parties and all the 'hoopla.' Either come to win or stay the hell home."

And win the Raiders did as Gene Upshaw helped bury the NFC Champion Minnesota Vikings, 32-14, before a live audience of more than 103,000 fans in the Rose Bowl and a world-wide television audience estimated at upward of 140 million people.

Gene Upshaw played in a club-record 217 league games for the Raiders, losing in only 55 of those. He started in 207 consecutive league games plus 24 post-season playoff games. He became the only player in NFL history to play in Super Bowls in three different decades—after the 1967, 1976 and 1980 seasons. Offensive captain for nine years—1973 thru 1981—he earned All-Pro or All-Conference honors eight times and played in six AFC-NFC Pro Bowls and earlier in one AFL All-Star Game.

Gene Upshaw was only the second player inducted into the Pro Football Hall of Fame who had played only offensive guard. During his memorable career, his Raiders made the playoffs 11 times and won two World Championships of Professional Football. Upshaw, now the executive director of the NFL Players Association, was named to the AFL-NFL 25-year All Star team and the NFL 75th Anniversary All-Time team. He was elected to the Hall of Fame in his first year of eligibility and enshrined on August 8, 1967.

From high school football in Erie, Pennsylvania, to college football in Tallahassee, Florida, to 14 winning seasons of professional football in Oakland, California, to a hallowed place in the Pro Football Hall of Fame in Canton, Ohio, everyone who described Fred Biletnikoff started by talking about his "hands."

"Great hands" or "sure hands" or "soft hands" or "quiet hands" are some of the expressions found in stories about the six-foot-one, 190 pound Biletnikoff who ranked fourth among all-time NFL receivers when he retired after the 1978 season.

Crediting the former Florida State University All-America with special hands is perhaps to give nature an undue emphasis and overlook the tremendous effort that earned greatness for Fred Biletnikoff.

As one Raider quarterback who teamed with Biletnikoff recalls, "Nobody worked as hard as Fred did. Heck, if he dropped a particular kind of pass in practice, first he cursed up a storm and then he bugged me to stay out with him after practice so he could run that same pattern again, again and again. He'd throw my arm out if I let him."

Hard work and athletic prowess, combined with intense desire and determination, were early parts of Fred Biletnikoff's drive for greatness. At Tech Memorial High School in Erie, he lettered not only in football but also in basketball and baseball and—yes—even track. At least part of the Biletnikoff legend of great hands but no speed was more myth than legend.

A writer once said about Biletnikoff, "He couldn't win a race with Minnesota Fats, but if you're looking for a guy who can get open in a subway rush, Fred owns the patent."

With speed not a specialty, Biletnikoff built his style on running precise routes, utilizing his quickness, learning all the tricks of his craft and developing a coachlike understanding of the passing game.

Hard work and attention to detail paid off big

for Biletnikoff. He set school career and single season records at Florida State for receptions, reception yardage, touchdown catches and points scored. He was chosen Most Valuable Player in the Gator Bowl Game after the 1964 college season as his Florida State team upset mighty Oklahoma. In that game, Biletnikoff caught 13 passes for 192 yards and four touchdowns. Understandably, he is a member of the all-time Gator Bowl All-Star Team.

Immediately upon the conclusion of that

marvelous performance in the Gator Bowl, Fred Biletnikoff signed his first pro football contract with the Oakland Raiders right under the goal posts. The Raiders had taken him in the second round of the AFL draft. With only eight teams in the league then, that was the equivalent of a very early first-round selection in today's 30-team drafts.

As a rookie with Oakland in 1965, Biletnikoff caught 24 passes and the Raiders had an 8-5-1 record. From '65 thru '78, he caught 589 passes in regular-season play, a Raider record that stood until broken by Tim Brown in the final game of the 1997 season. In addition, Biletnikoff caught 70 more passes in postseason games. And the Oakland Raiders never had a single losing season in those 14 years that

Fred Biletnikoff lined up at his familiar wide receiver post.

In 1976 postseason action, Fred Biletnikoff caught nine passes in the Raiders thrilling, come-from-behind 24-21 victory over the New England Patriots in the AFC Playoff Game. Three weeks later in Super Bowl XI he was named Most Valuable Player after three of his catches set up short touchdown runs in the Raiders 32-14 win over the Minnesota Vikings.

During Biletnikoff's 14 years in Silver and Black, the Raiders earned a 144-45-9 record, won their way into the playoffs 10 times, won the AFL Championship, the AFC Championship, were in two Super Bowls and won the World Championship of Professional Football. Fred had twenty-one 100-yard games in the regular season, then four more during the playoffs. He had 10 consecutive seasons with 40 or more catches in those years of 14-game seasons. He led the Raiders in pass receptions for six consecutive seasons and led the entire league in 1971.

Fred Biletnikoff played in two AFL All-Star Games and four AFC-NFC Pro Bowl Games. He was All-Pro or All-Conference five straight seasons.

But records alone don't single out Fred Biletnikoff for the great respect he won from teammates and competitors alike. It was the grace and skills of the many one-handed scoring catches in the end zone corners of the Oakland Coliseum, the gravity-defying toe-tapping along the sidelines to come down in-bounds and earn another clutch first down. It was these courageous one-on-one challenges with the most talented cornerbacks in professional football. These brilliant duels brought out the best in Fred Biletnikoff, who caught most of his 76 touchdowns passes against tight man-to-man coverage. Then the hands came into play—but these were never really as important as the head—and the heart.

With the enshrinement of former Raider offensive tackle Art Shell into the Pro Football Hall of Fame on August 5, 1989, the finest single side of an offensive line in the eight decades of professional football history was joined again in the hallowed home of the game's greatest. At center—Jim Otto. At left guard—Gene Upshaw. And now, at left tackle—Art Shell.

Art Shell was the third of this superlative trio to join the Raiders, coming aboard as a third-round draft choice in 1968 out of Maryland State College (now known as the University of Maryland—Eastern Shore).

Jim Otto had arrived from the University of Miami in 1960 as an undersized center. Gene Upshaw arrived from Texas A&I University in 1967, with the sleek, sculptured body that would soon change the look at guard in professional football. Art Shell arrived in Oakland as a massive young man with the body of a giant, the heart of a warrior and the pride that epitomizes the Raider motto of "Pride and Poise."

Some pro scouts labeled Art Shell as being "soft," or "having a weight problem" or being "untested against real competition." But the Oakland Raider scouting operation—labeled by Newsweek magazine as "one part genius, one part fanatic and one part CIA"—felt that this third-round pick would develop into a great player.

The test of time again proved the astuteness of Raider judgement. "Big Art" went on to play in 207 league games, missing only five games thru injury during his 15 active seasons.

Art Shell was chosen to play in eight Pro Bowls—a number untopped by any Raider player thru 1997. He played in 23 postseason games, including eight AFL or AFC Championship Games and in Raider victories in Super Bowls XI and XV.

A two-way tackle in college, Art Shell was

offense all the way once he came to Oakland. From 1968 thru 1978, Art Shell played in 156 consecutive league games. A preseason injury in 1979 kept him out of the first five league games of that season—the only games he ever missed. Then, with the sixth game of the '79 regular season, Art Shell began a streak of 51 more games before retiring to join the Raider coaching staff in 1983.

During his 207-game span the Raiders lost only 53 times. And when Hall of Fame inductees Art Shell, Gene Upshaw and Jim Otto played side-by-side, the Oakland Raider record was 71-20-7.

One outstanding NFL defensive lineman, referring to his battles over the years against Art Shell, said, "He not only blocked me, he blocked out the sun. God, he hit hard, but always clean."

Lyle Alzado once said that, "The hardest I've

ever been hit was by Art Shell in my first full-contact drill after coming to the Raiders in 1982. I think he was just letting me know who owned the turf around here. It was one helluva way to be welcomed." Intense pride was a key to Art Shell's success. Coach John Madden had given him a job—protect our quarterbacks. And Art Shell believed in doing his job, of earning his way. He did not want to be beaten. He just would not tolerate it.

On January 9, 1977, in Super Bowl XI against the NFC Champion Minnesota Vikings, Art Shell pitched the offensive lineman's equivalent of a "no hitter." Facing highly regarded Viking defensive end Jim Marshall—a key member of Minnesota's famed "Purple People Eaters," Shell shut his man out, allowing no tackles, no assists and no quarterback sacks as the Silver and Black totally dominated the Vikings, 32-14 to win Super Bowl XI and the World Championship of Professional Football. The Raiders that day gained a record-breaking 439 yards on offense.

Number 78—the great Art Shell—did his job quietly, and superbly. For running backs such as Marv Hubbard, Clarence Davis, Mark van Eeghen, Charlie Smith, Pete Banaszak and others, he cleared a path thru the best of defenses, paving their way with mind and muscle, class and courage, pride and performance.

Number 78—the great Art Shell—kept ferocious pass rushers off the likes of Daryle Lamonica, George Blanda, Ken Stabler and Jim Plunkett. The Raider vertical passing game demands much more of its pass blockers than does any other system as the ball is often held longer and the running backs are often out in the patterns as possible receivers rather than held in to protect. But Art Shell accepted this challenge and mastered it.

Art Shell did more than come to play. He came to excel. He came to be the best. He came to win—and he did!

38

What can you expect from a tall, skinny mathematics major who took courses in electromagnetic theory and differential equations, owned his own limousine, spoke fluent Spanish and earned four Super Bowl rings while playing linebacker for 215 regular-season games for three different National Football League teams?

Well, if you're the Raiders—the last of the three teams he played for during 15 years in the pros—you list Theodore Paul Hendricks among those wearing the famed Silver and Black who have earned enshrinement in the Pro Football Hall of Fame.

People who begin a description of Ted Hendricks by itemizing his eccentricities miss the point. He wasn't elected to the Hall of Fame because of his sense of humor or his colorful, unique lifestyle. No, indeed! Ted Hendricks earned his spot in this very exclusive group of greats of the game by his extraordinary accomplishments on the field from 1969 thru 1983, with the Baltimore Colts (1969-73), Green Bay Packers (1974) and Oakland/Los Angeles Raiders (1975-83).

Playing 215 consecutive games at linebacker—as physically challenging a position as there is in professional football—is a monumental accomplishment. Playing in eight Pro Bowls is a measure of the respect in which Ted Hendricks was held by NFL players and coaches who vote to select Pro Bowl performers.

In his 15 seasons Hendricks blocked 25 field goals or extra points. He sacked quarterbacks frequently but these didn't become an "official" statistic until 1982. He blocked passes. He intercepted passes—26 to be exact. He made tackles along the line, downfield and in the backfield. And on an NFL-record four occasions he made the play in the end zone to record safeties. He recovered 16 fumbles. He scored one touchdown on a pass interception return, another on a blocked punt return and a third on a fumble return. Not bad defense for a guy who started as a quarterback in high school.

Ted Hendricks had some personal rules for playing that may have affected his longevity. "Don't stand around pile-ups. Don't go to the ground unnecessarily. Avoid intrasquad scrimmages and training camp scrimmages against other teams…," and more. But when plays had to be made, all the rules were down the drain and there was six-foot-seven of ferocious linebacker right in the middle of the action.

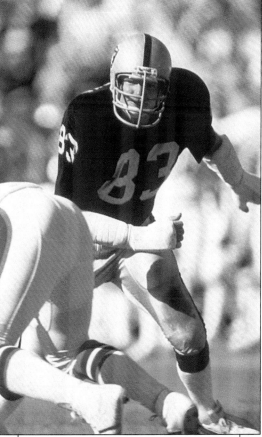

Ted Hendricks was in the playoffs nine times and on four Super Bowl teams, including all three World Championship triumphs with the Raiders. Earlier, he had played in Super Bowl V with the Baltimore Colts, who had drafted him in round two of the 1969 NFL draft.

Hendricks played his high school football in Hialeah, Florida, then went to the University of Miami where he was a three-time All-America choice as a defensive end. But he lasted until the second round of the draft as clubs were uncertain about where he would play as a pro. Wasn't he too skinny at 214 pounds to be a defensive end and too long-legged at six-foot-seven to be an outside backer? Could he keep blockers from getting to his legs and cutting him?

Well, people tried to cut him. They tried for 15 years. They tried for 215 league games and four Super Bowls. They tried—and they failed!

Ted Hendricks had long arms, exceptional use of his hands and great balance and agility. He used leverage to make it impossible to get underneath his arms and chop him. Blockers did not get to his feet. They ended on the ground as he worked into another tackle.

A legendary practical joker, Ted Hendricks was serious as a football player. He possessed rare instincts as to what an opponent could and could not do. Turned loose in some Raiders defensive alignments, he distorted an offensive game plan. Offenses had to know where he was lined up and had to account for him. As he moved and shifted they had to adjust blocking schemes, then try to readjust when he relocated.

Cincinnati Bengals running back Boobie Clark summed up some of the problems Hendricks created. "I just hate it when I have to try to block him. I mean he really moves around. And if you do get to him he pounds you with those arms. And he's so quick he's gone before you realize it."

One uncanny thing about Hendricks' defensive play was his ability to position himself to create the biggest possible problem. Uncommon plays—the leaping interception, the long reach for a tackle, the ability to get off the block—these became the ordinary for Hendricks.

As then-Raider assistant coach Charlie Sumner said about Hendricks during the 1980 Super Bowl season, "At least once a game he'll do something great and I won't know how he did it."

It wasn't by accident that Ted Hendricks made those remarkable plays—and it was not by accident that he is one of the few outside linebackers enshrined in the Pro Football Hall of Fame.

"Probably the most technically sound defensive back in pro football history," said one veteran NFL executive. "The very best example of how to play comerback I've ever seen," said a long-time NFL coach, adding, "If you could make a film of how he played pass defense, it would be the best teaching device to show your young players I can think of."

This is how some of pro football's most experienced, most respected talent evaluators describe corner-back Mike Haynes, the latest great Raider inducted into the Professional Football Hall of Fame.

Mike Haynes, who played on the corner for 14 seasons—the first seven with the New England Patriots and the final seven with the Los Angeles Raiders—was enshrined in the Hall of Fame on July 26, 1997.

A Denison, Texas native, Haynes began his football career at John Marshall High School in Los Angeles where he was an outstanding football player and one of the state's top track athletes as a long jumper as well. His leadership skills were also an apparent area as he captained the football team as a senior and was voted Senior Athlete of the Year.

Next stop for Michael James Haynes was Arizona State University where he again starred in both football and track. He was a two-year letterman in track, winning the conference championship in the long jump. In football he was an All-America defensive back as both a junior and senior, a three time All Conference selection as a defensive back and punt returner. Haynes was named Most Valuable Player in the 1973 Fiesta Bowl and Most Valuable Defensive Player in the 1976 Japan Bowl. Again, as a senior, he was team captain.

The New England Patriots selected Mike Haynes with the fifth pick and as the first defensive back taken in the first round of the 1976 NFL college player draft. With eight pass interceptions and a 13-yard average per punt return that '76 season, it came as no surprise when he was named AFC Rookie of the Year and went to the Pro Bowl as a rookie. During his seven seasons with the Patriots, 1976-1982, Haynes was selected for the Pro Bowl six times.

In the spring of 1983, Mike Haynes became a free agent, and, after a legal battle, he joined the Raiders in November of 1983. He played in the final five games of that season for the Raiders, and then in the three postseason games. He had a superb performance in Super Bowl XVIII as the Silver and Black secondary totally shut down the wide receivers of the Redskins as the Raiders dominated Washington, 38-9, to win their third World

Championship of Professional Football in an eight-year span.

Mike Haynes went on to play seven years for the Raiders, 1983-1989. He finished his illustrious pro career with 46 pass interceptions including two returned for touchdowns and a total of 668 yards on interception returns. His 97-yard interception return against the Miami Dolphins on December 2, 1984 is the second longest such return in Raider history.

Nine times during his pro football career Mike Haynes was chosen by the players and coaches in the league to play in the Pro Bowl.

"Mike Haynes was the smoothest, most graceful corner-back I've ever seen in this league," said one NFL head coach. "He just makes everything so easy."

His play may have looked "easy" but no one worked harder to physically and mentally prepare for a season, a game, a particular receiver than did the six-foot-two, 190 pound Mike Haynes. He had great pride in his physical condition, in his work ethic, in his efforts—and in the results of all this preparation.

One of the best receivers in the AFC West once described Mike Haynes as "your dance partner when you go out in the pattern. He will match you step for step, move for move, shake for shake. You're just not going to get loose. It's frustrating as hell."

Smooth, graceful, quick, fast—yes, all of those. But Mike Haynes was also tough, intense, intelligent. Pride and Poise and Commitment to Excellence were never idle phrases to this great cornerback. He wore the famed Silver and Black with class and distinction all the way from California to the Pro Football Hall of Fame in Canton, Ohio—the proper depository for that black jersey with the silver number 22.

Raider owner Al Davis justly earned his hallowed place in the Professional Football Hall of Fame with great accomplishments during a truly remarkable career in pro football. Al Davis is enshrined as one of only 193 people so honored in the 79 years during which the National Football League has

missioner and team owner.

The litany of Davis' accomplishments in meeting—and conquering—these varied challenges is well-known, but there are many other fascinating contributions made by Al Davis that are not nearly as recognized.

When Al Davis, just in his early twenties,

service powerhouse football team that went on to defeat the national college champion University of Maryland team in a squad game. A number of players from that Fort Belvoir squad—his first as a head coach—were in attendance in Canton, Ohio on August 1, 1992, nearly 40 years later, when Davis was enshrined

been in operation. Even more rare is being one of only two dozen or so coaches, administrators, executives or league commissioners chosen for this most exclusive of groups. So few who did so much for the game they loved.

The magnificent four decades in which the Raiders, led by Al Davis—first as head coach and general manager, next as managing general partner and finally as owner and chief executive officer—became professional sports winningest team are a chronicle of never-equaled achievements. Al Davis is the only man in this sport to have been an assistant coach, head coach, scout, general manager, league com-

was an assistant coach at Adelphi College on Long Island, New York, he wrote a number of very sound, analytical articles dealing with various technical phases of football for the leading coaching trade manuals—"Scholastic Coach Magazine" and "Athletic Journal." These articles became topics of conversations within the coaching profession and led to Davis' frequent selection to lecture at football coaching clinics throughout the country.

Later, while on active duty with the United States Army, Al Davis was named head football coach at the Army Engineering Center at Fort Belvoir, Virginia. There he developed a ranking

in the Professional Football Hall of Fame. Al Davis' legendary loyalty had begun very early in his career.

At 24 years of age, Al Davis worked with the NFL Baltimore Colts, primarily in player personnel. There he was associated closely with a crafty, cunning veteran of the football wars— Colts director of player personnel, Keith Molesworth. The "Admiral," as he was known, was an astute teacher. Al Davis was a very willing student.

It was then off to the Citadel Military College in Charleston, South Carolina as an assistant coach and chief recruiter. A number of phases of the "no huddle" or "quick huddle" offenses now in vogue in the NFL were forecast by the "race horse football" first developed by Al Davis at the Citadel.

In the final years of the '50s, Al Davis served on the football staff at the University of Southern California, under head coach Don Clark—one of the finest men to have ever been involved in sports. That USC team included a pair of athletes who went on to be enshrined in the Pro Football Hall of Fame—offensive tackle Ron Mix and defensive back Willie Wood. Also on that outstanding coaching staff with Al Davis was another Pro Football Hall of Fame member, Mel Hein—a great center and linebacker for the New York Giants in the '30s and '40s. Hein would later be hired as Director of Officials for the American Football League by Al Davis when Davis was asked by AFL owners to leave coaching and become Commissioner of the American Football League.

Al Davis was a pioneer in the AFL, having been hired by Los Angeles Chargers head coach Sid Gillman to help start the new team and work with the passing game. The Pro Football Hall of Fame connection continued as Gillman was later voted in and another young assistant from that staff, Chuck Noll, was also so honored at a later date.

Among the great players Al Davis recruited and coached with the Chargers was superlative wide receiver Lance Alworth, who later chose Davis to make the presentation speech when he was enshrined in the Hall of Fame. Alworth was just the first of eight great players to have named Al Davis to present them when inducted into the Pro Football Hall of Fame.

In 1963, Al Davis moved from the champi-

onship-quality Chargers in San Diego to the struggling Raiders in Oakland as head coach and general manager. He quickly created order out of chaos and came within one game of the championship, going 10-4-0 in that first season.

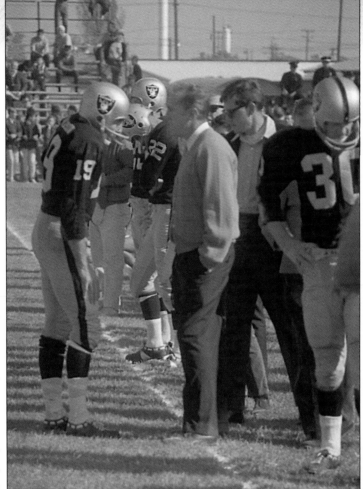

"Bump and run" coverage—a pass defense principle Al Davis developed after watching John Wooden, legendary basketball coach of UCLA, employ tight, pressing, one-on-one defensive tactics—was just one of many innovations he brought to the game. Off-season mini-camps, strength and conditioning programs, three-man defensive fronts, employing two wide receivers on the same side of the formation are examples of different phases of the pioneering approach.

Al Davis was also a pioneer in another very significant area—the employment of members of minorities in major positions not before available to these underrepresented groups.

Tom Flores was the first Hispanic-American head coach in the National Football League. Art Shell was the first African-American to serve as an NFL head coach in the modern era. Many other examples of this awareness of such needs exist, pointing out why Al Davis was recently named "the Branch Rickey of football" by a leading African-American publication.

As a member of the NFL's Competition Committee, responsible for the playing rules and personnel policies of the pro game, Al Davis continued to be one of the most creative and influential members of the league.

The Raiders under Al Davis have won the American Football League Championship, three American Football Conference Championships and three World Championships of Professional Football. They have had 69 different players chosen to play in the NFL Pro Bowl or the AFL All-Star Game. They have had nine people enshrined in the Pro Football Hall of Fame. They have won or shared 14 division championships in the toughest division in the NFL. They have been in the playoffs in 18 different seasons. At one point, they had 16 consecutive winning seasons. At one point, they scored in 217 consecutive games.

In the four decades Al Davis has directed the Raiders, they have become the most respected, most imitated and most feared organization in professional sports.

The Raiders under Al Davis have had the greatest players, the greatest coaches, the greatest plays and played in the greatest games in the history of professional football. This is a legacy of Pro Football Hall of Fame member Al Davis, for "GREAT MEN INSPIRE IN OTHERS THE WILL TO BE GREAT."

RAIDERS IN THE PRO BOWL

RAIDERS IN THE AFC-NFC PRO BOWL, 1970-1997

MARCUS ALLEN	RB	5	(1982, 84, 85, 86*, 87)
FRED BILETNIKOFF	WR	4	(1970, 71, 73, 74)
CLIFF BRANCH	WR	4	(1974, 75, 76, 77)
BOB BROWN	T	1	(1971*)
TIM BROWN	WR/KR	7	(1988, 91, 93, 94, 95, 96, 97)
WILLIE BROWN	CB	4	(1970, 71, 72, 73)
DAVE CASPER	TE	4	(1976, 77, 78, 79)
RAYMOND CHESTER	TE	4	(1970, 71, 72, 79)
TODD CHRISTENSEN	TE	5	(1983, 84, 85, 86, 87)
DAVE DALBY	C	1	(1977)
HEWRITT DIXON	RB	1	(1970)
KEVIN GOGAN	G	1	(1994)
JEFF GOSSETT	P	1	(1991)
RAY GUY	P	7	(1973, 74, 75, 76, 77, 78, 80)
LESTER HAYES	CB	5	(1980, 81, 82, 83, 84)
MIKE HAYNES	CB	3	(1984, 85, 86)
TED HENDRICKS	LB	4	(1980, 81, 82, 83)
ETHAN HORTON	TE	1	(1991)
JEFF HOSTETLER	QB	1	(1994)
MARV HUBBARD	RB	3	(1971, 72, 73)
BO JACKSON	RB	1	(1990*)
KENNY KING	RB	1	(1980*)
JEFF JAEGER	K	1	(1991)
DARYLE LAMONICA	QB	2	(1970, 72)
HENRY LAWRENCE	T	2	(1983, 84)
HOWIE LONG	DE	8	(1983, 84, 85, 86, 87, 89, 92, 93)
RONNIE LOTT	S	1	(1991)
ROD MARTIN	LB	2	(1983, 84)
TERRY McDANIEL	CB	5	(1992, 93, 94, 95, 96)
VANN McELROY	S	2	(1983, 84)
CHESTER McGLOCKTON	DT	4	(1994, 95, 96, 97)
MATT MILLEN	LB	1	(1988)
MAX MONTOYA	G	1	(1993)
DON MOSEBAR	C	3	(1986, 90, 91)
JIM OTTO	C	3	(1970, 71, 72)
GREG PRUITT	KR	1	(1983)
HARRY SCHUH	T	1	(1970)
ART SHELL	T	8	(1972, 73, 74, 75, 76, 77, 78, 80)
OTIS SISTRUNK	DT	1	(1974)
KEN STABLER	QB	4	(1973, 74, 76*, 77)
JACK TATUM	S	3	(1973, 74, 75*)
GREG TOWNSEND	DE	2	(1990, 91)
GENE UPSHAW	G	6	(1972, 73, 74, 75, 76, 77)
MARK VAN EEGHEN	RB	1	(1977)
PHIL VILLAPIANO	LB	4	(1973, 74, 75, 76)
WARREN WELLS	WR	1	(1970)
STEVE WISNIEWSKI	G	7	(1990, 91, 92*, 93, 94*, 95, 97)

*Selected, but did not play

Howie Long

Art Shell

Tim Brown

Ray Guy

Steve Wisniewski

Gene Upshaw

RAIDERS IN THE AFL ALL-STAR GAME, 1961-69

GEORGE ATKINSON	CB	2	(1968,1969)	TOM KEATING	DT	2	(1966,67)
FRED BILETNIKOFF	WR	2	(1967,69)	DARYLE LAMONICA	QB	2	(1967,69)
DAN BIRDWELL	DT	1	(1968)	ISSAC LASSITER	DE	1	(1966)
GEORGE BLANDA	K	1	(1967)	ARCHIE MATSOS	LB	1	(1963)
WILLIE BROWN	CB	3	(1967,68,69)	KENT McCLOUGHAN	CB	2	(1966,67)
BILLY CANNON	TE	1	(1969)	ALAN MILLER	RB	1	(1961)
DAN CONNERS	LB	3	(1966,67,68)	GUS OTTO	LB	1	(1969)
DAVE COSTA	DT	1	(1963)	JIM OTTO	C	9	(1961,62,63 64,
CLEM DANIELS	RB	4	(1963,64,65,66)				65,66,67,68,69)
BEN DAVIDSON	DE	3	(1966,67,68)	ART POWELL	WR	4	(1963,64,65,66)
COTTON DAVIDSON	QB	1	(1963)	HARRY SCHUH	T	2	(1967,69)
HEWRITT DIXON	RB	3	(1966,67,68)	GENE UPSHAW	G	1	(1968)
TOM FLORES	QB	1	(1966)	WARREN WELLS	WR	1	(1968)
DAVE GRAYSON	CB-S	3	(1965,66,67)	FRED WILLIAMSON	CB	3	(1961,62,63)
WAYNE HAWKINS	G	5	(1963,64,65,66,67)	NEMIAH WILSON	CB	1	(1967)

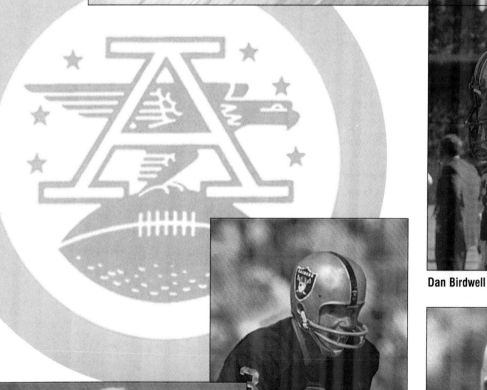

Dan Birdwell

Daryle Lamonica

Jim Otto   Clem Daniels

At the conclusion of each college season the famed Heisman Trophy is awarded by the New York Athletic Club to the best player in college football as selected by a national panel.

The great moment of winning the Heisman Trophy has happened to seven college stars who went on to wear the Silver and Black of the Raiders.

BILLY CANNON, first of the Raiders' Heisman Trophy winners, was a great running back at Louisiana State University in the late fifties, before being drafted after the 1959 campaign by the Houston Oilers of the newly formed A m e r i c a n Football League. Cannon played running back for four seasons with Houston, helping them win the first two AFL Championships in 1960 and 1961. He was acquired by the Oakland Raiders in 1964 in one of the earliest in a series of aggressive

Billy Cannon

first of four World Championship Games for the Silver and Black.

JIM PLUNKETT led Stanford University to a Rose Bowl victory before being voted Heisman Trophy winner after the 1970 college season. He was the very first player taken in the 1971 NFL draft, going to the New England Patriots where he was the starting quarterback as a rookie. He was traded to the San Francisco 49ers in 1976 where he struggled for two seasons on a rebuilding team, finally being waived in the 1978 preseason. Shortly thereafter Al Davis signed Plunkett as a free agent. Plunkett didn't throw a pass in '78 and only 15 in '79 as he rebuilt his confidence as well as his body. Then, in 1980, Plunkett moved in as the starter when Dan Pastorini went out with a season ending injury in the fifth game, with the Raiders off to a 2-3-0 start. With Plunkett under center, the Raiders won 13 of their next 15 games, including three playoff contests plus a Super Bowl XV triumph over the favored NFC Champion Philadelphia Eagles, 27-10, in the Louisiana Superdome in New Orleans. Plunkett led the Raiders into these 1980 playoffs as a "wild-card" team and emerged as

another World Championship with a dominating 38-9 victory over the NFC Champion Washington Redskins.

MARCUS ALLEN, college football's top player in 1981 as tailback for USC, was a rare rookie starter for the relocated Los Angeles Raiders as the organization's first-round draft choice in 1982. A year later the multitalented Allen had rushed for over 1,000 yards in the regular season, and his 191 yards rushing in Super Bowl XVIII earned him the game's MVP Award as the powerful Raiders crushed the NFC Champion Washington Redskins, 38-9, in Tampa Stadium in Tampa, Florida. Allen set numerous Raider and NFL records while with the Silver and Black thru the 1992 season—

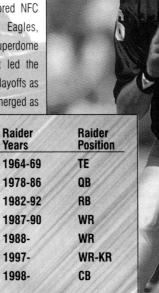

Heisman Year	Player	College Position	College	Raider Years	Raider Position
1959	BILLY CANNON	RB	LSU	1964-69	TE
1970	JIM PLUNKETT	QB	STANFORD	1978-86	QB
1981	MARCUS ALLEN	RB	USC	1982-92	RB
1985	BO JACKSON	RB	AUBURN	1987-90	WR
1987	TIM BROWN	RB-WR	NOTRE DAME	1988-	WR
1991	DESMOND HOWARD	WR-KR	MICHIGAN	1997-	WR-KR
1997	CHARLES WOODSON	CB-WR	MICHIGAN	1998-	CB

trades and signings made by head coach-general manager Al Davis to put his Raiders ahead of the pack. Eventually converted to tight end by Davis, Cannon went on to post Raider career stats of 134 receptions for 2,268 yards and 25 touchdowns. The former LSU great started for the Raiders in Super Bowl II—the

Super Bowl Most Valuable Player as quarterback of the new World Champions. Again, in 1983, Plunkett helped the Raiders thunder into the playoffs with a 12-4-0 record, as the Silver and Black won

Jim Plunkett

Marcus Allen

including a league best of 11 consecutive 100-yards rushing games. He finished his 11 seasons with the Raiders as team leader in rushing yardage (8,545), rushes (2,090), rushing touchdowns (79), touchdowns (95) and the single-season mark of 1,759 yards rushing in 1985. Allen finished his Raider career with 22 100-yard rushing games plus three 100-yard pass receiving games before joining the Kansas City Chiefs in 1993.

BO JACKSON, voted the best college football player in 1985 for his achievements at Auburn University, has been widely acclaimed for his remarkable physical attributes. But an unyielding will to win was a key to his success in all his athletic endeavors. Originally selected as the first player in the NFL draft in 1986, Jackson opted to play baseball instead. Eligible again for the NFL draft in '87 while playing baseball, he was chosen by the Raiders in

round seven and then fooled everyone—except Al Davis and the Raiders—by signing to play football once his baseball season with the Kansas City Royals ended. Jackson immediately made his mark in the NFL, receiving Rookie of the Year honors after averaging 6.8 yards per carry and a record-setting 221-yard, three-touchdown performance in a Monday night victory in Seattle. In four baseball-shortened seasons with the Raiders, Bo Jackson set a club carrer rushing record of 5.4 yards per carry and became the only ball carrier in NFL history to have two runs from scrimmage of over 90 yards. Jackson is also the only player in the history of the two sports to have been chosen to play in both the NFL Pro Bowl and the Major League Baseball All-Star Game. Participating in only 35 Raider league games before a hip injury ended his football career, Bo Jackson rushed for 2,782 yards on just 515 carries.

TIM BROWN, winner of the 1987 Heisman Trophy when he led Notre Dame as a receiver, running back, punt and kickoff returner, was the first of three Raider first-round picks in 1988. He made an immediate impression with a 97-yard kickoff return for a score in his first NFL game. Tim Brown set an NFL rookie record for total

yardage of 2,316 yards on pass receptions, rushing, kickoff returns and punt returns. A 75-yard punt return for a TD against Cincinnati in '91 made him the only Raider to have ever scored on both a punt return and kickoff return. With 80 receptions in '93, back-to-back 89 reception seasons in '94 and '95 and 90 catches in 1996—most ever by a Raider wide receiver—Brown moved into third place among all-time Raider pass catchers. With 104 receptions in 1997 Tim Brown had 599 catches in his career—most ever by a Raider receiver.

DESMOND HOWARD, selected as college football's best in 1991 and awarded the Heisman Trophy as he starred for the University of Michigan as a receiver, ball carrier, punt and kickoff returner. He set various NCAA records before coming into the NFL in 1992 as Washington Redskins first-round draft choice. An All-Rookie selection in '92, he became a starter in 1994 before being acquired by the Jacksonville Jaguars in the NFL expansion draft prior to the '95 campaign. He signed with the

Bo Jackson

Green Bay Packers for 1996 and set the NFL single season punt return-yardage record and led the league in punt-return average. He also led the NFL with three punts returned for touchdowns, second-most in a single season in league history. Super Bowl XXXI Most Valuable

Black. As a three year starter at cornerback at the University of Michigan from 1995 thru 1997, Charles Woodson became the first predominately defensive player to ever win this prestigious award as the best player in college football. Since the Heisman Trophy was first awarded in 1936, no other defender has been honored in this manner. Though used as a wide receiver and/or running back on occasion, as well as a punt returner, Woodson made his mark as a tenacious pass defender and a tough support man against the run. An All-Big Ten Conference first-team choice in both his freshman and sophomore season, Woodson was a unanimous All American and All Conference pick as a junior in 1997 while helping Michigan win the Conference Championship, the Rose Bowl and a share of the NCAA Football Championship. The Fremont, Ohio native was Michigan's Most Valuable Player in 1997, among a vast array of postseason honors and awards. The Raiders selected Woodson as their first-round draft pick in April, 1998, making him the fourth player chosen in the draft and the very first defensive back selected.

These seven great athletes—Billy Cannon, Jim Plunkett, Marcus Allen, Bo Jackson, Tim Brown, Desmond Howard, and Charles Woodson—from six great universities—LSU, Stanford, USC, Auburn, Notre Dame and Michigan—had two great experiences in common: winning the Heisman Trophy and playing for the Raiders.

Tim Brown

Desmond Howard

Player after totaling 244 return yards, including a 99-yard kickoff return for a touchdown to seal the Packers win. He was the first player ever to be voted a Super Bowl MVP as a special teams player. With Oakland he led the NFL in kickoff return yardage in 1997.

CHARLES WOODSON, most recent Heisman Trophy winner to join the Silver and

Charles Woodson

Sound hits you at a speed of 760 mph. Light hits you at a speed of 671,000,000 mph. Toshiba DVD makes it actually feel like it.

Your pulse races. Your gut quivers. That little vein in your forehead is throbbing. Senses—meet Toshiba DVD.

PLEASE, NO TALKING DURING THE SHOW

At Toshiba, we've developed the technology that fits up to 133 minutes of heart-pounding video and audio, normally reserved for the finest cineplexes, for use at home on a disc the size of a CD. Picture quality that's three times better than VHS and audio recorded in full Dolby Digital Surround Sound® on six discrete channels. And, our models can even play your favorite compact discs.

5" (same as CD)

NO WAITING, NO FADING, NO RENOVATING

Because the discs are read by laser, there is never any need to rewind a DVD. And, there's no chance of your favorite DVD deteriorating with every play like a VHS tape. Finally, you won't have to build an addition to your home to hold your DVDs. The packages are as streamlined and efficient as the discs themselves.

TALL, SHORT, OR FRENCH— WE'RE READY FOR ANYTHING

Many DVD movies will come with some of the most incredible options only Hollywood and Toshiba could dream of, including the ability to change the format of the movie to fit any television you play it through, from regular size to widescreen; language tracks of up to eight different languages ranging from English to French; subtitles in up to 32 different languages; the ability to view the same scene of a movie from any of up to nine remote-controlled angles; or multiple endings to the same movie. If the feature is on the disc, Toshiba DVD players are ready for it.

YEAH, SO?

We believe your senses will thank you for this complete and total assault. As soon as they're out of traction.

Toshiba DVD

You've got senses. Use them.

For more information, call 1-800-346-6672.

Gene Upshaw

Jim Otto

A few years ago, a writer asked Raiders executive assistant Al LoCasale what the organization looks for in a top draft choice. Among other things the answer included this comment:

"He should be somebody whose name we put in the starting lineup early in his career and then we leave it there for 10-12 years."

Meticulous planning for the draft, outstanding medical care over the years, excellent training and conditioning programs, the best in facilities and equipment and athletes who genuinely care, have made such a definition an accurate one for the Raiders.

Over the decades a number of Raiders have lined up, played hard and won for ten years or longer. But there is a very special group of five who played in more than 200 league games for the Raider organization:

217	GENE UPSHAW	G	1967-1982
210	JIM OTTO	C	1960-1974
207	RAY GUY	P	1973-1986
207	ART SHELL	T	1968-1982
205	DAVE DALBY	C	1972-1985

These five great athletes played in 1,046 league games for the Raiders. That's one thousand forty six games in places like frozen Buffalo or hot, humid Miami, at mile-high Denver or below sea-level New Orleans. In domes, on grass, on dirt, on ice, in rain or snow. That's when well or sick, prime or aching, rested or tired, whatever, whenever and wherever.

Truly, this quintet of gridiron greats served above and beyond the call of duty. These five helped establish standards by which the true greatness of the Raiders is measured, in the past, in the present and in the future.

Ray Guy

Dave Dalby

Art Shell

For every deadline, a finish line.

In business, you don't always have to come in first to win. You just have to come up with the right solution at the right time. That's why UPS offers a whole range of guaranteed, on-time delivery options.* More than anyone else, in fact. It's part of our commitment to meeting the demands of your business. And a good example of why when it comes to helping you be more competitive, there's really no competition.

UPS

MOVING at the SPEED *of* BUSINESS.™

NFL™
Official Package
Delivery Company

www.ups.com • 1-800-PICK-UPS

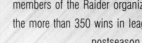
W hile statistics are never the true measure of a man, they can be used to measure a man's accomplishments.

The most important single number to members of the Raider organization is the more than 350 wins in league and postseason games that have been earned by the mind and muscle, sinew and sweat of the 600 or so athletes who have worn the hallowed Silver and Black since 1960.

But individual statistics do help keep great moments alive and fresh. We now list record setting single game performances that again demonstrate the Raider traditions of the greatest players, the greatest coaches, the greatest plays and the greatest games in the annals of professional sports.

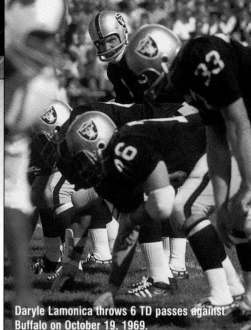

Daryle Lamonica throws 6 TD passes against Buffalo on October 19, 1969.

RAIDER INDIVIDUAL SINGLE GAME RECORDS

MOST POINTS SCORED
24 by Art Powell (12-26-63 vs Houston Oilers)
24 by Marcus Allen (9-24-84 vs San Diego Chargers)

MOST FIELD GOALS MADE
5 by Jeff Jaeger (12-11-94 vs Denver Broncos)

LONGEST FIELD GOAL MADE
54 yards by George Fleming (10-2-61 vs Denver Broncos)

MOST PASS COMPLETIONS
34 by Jim Plunkett (9-12-85 at Kansas City Chiefs)

MOST YARDS GAINED PASSING
424 by Jeff Hostetler (10-18-93 vs San Diego Chargers)

MOST TOUCHDOWN PASSES
6 by Tom Flores (12-22-63 vs Houston Oilers)
6 by Daryle Lamonica (10-19-69 vs Buffalo Bills)

BEST COMPLETION PERCENTAGE
91.7 by Ken Stabler (10-16-77 vs Denver Broncos)

LONGEST PASS PLAY
99 yards by Jim Plunkett to Cliff Branch
(10-2-83 at Washington Redskins)

MOST RUSHING ATTEMPTS
36 by Mark van Eeghen (10-23-77 at New York Jets)

MOST YARDS RUSHING
227 by Napoleon Kaufman (10-19-97 vs Denver Broncos)

BEST AVERAGE PER RUSH
14.6 yards by Bo Jackson (12-16-90 vs Cincinnati Bengals)

LONGEST RUN FROM SCRIMMAGE
92 yards by Bo Jackson (11-5-89 vs Cincinnati Bengals)

MOST PASS RECEPTIONS
14 by Tim Brown (12-21-97 vs Jacksonville Jaguars)

MOST YARDS ON RECEPTIONS
247 by Art Powell (12-22-63 vs Houston Oilers)

MOST TOUCHDOWN RECEPTIONS
4 by Art Powell (12-22-63 vs Houston Oilers)

LONGEST PUNT RETURN
97 yards by Greg Pruitt (10-2-83 at Washington Redskins)

LONGEST KICKOFF RETURN
104 yards by Ira Matthews (10-25-79 vs San Diego Chargers)

LONGEST INTERCEPTION RETURN
102 yards by Eddie Anderson (12-14-92 at Miami Dolphins)

LONGEST FUMBLE RETURN
104 yards by Jack Tatum (9-24-72 at Green Bay Packers)

LONGEST PUNT
77 yards by Wayne Crow (10-29-61 vs New York Titans)

Bo Jackson's 92 yard run vs. Cincinnati on November 5, 1989.

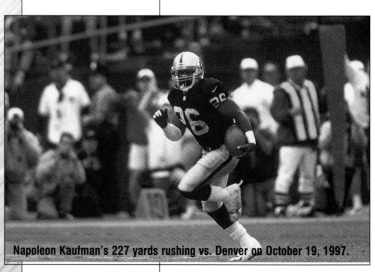

Napoleon Kaufman's 227 yards rushing vs. Denver on October 19, 1997.

When it comes to **paper,** there's only one **champion.**

We're proud that the Oakland Raiders Yearbook is printed on Champion papers. Champion is one of America's leading manufacturers of paper for business communications, commercial printing and publications, as well as a major producer of plywood and lumber.

 **Champion**
Champion International Corporation

The pro football college player draft has grown into a major event, with live television coverage, a library of special publications about the draft and thousands of articles in newspapers and magazines locally, regionally, nationally and internationally.

There are draft day parties, draft choice contests and unbelievable interest in the process by which pro football teams choose their new personnel from the college ranks.

The present 30 National Football League teams collectively spend millions of dollars and countless thousands of hours collecting the information to make these key personnel decisions. Binoculars, stop watches, measuring tapes, IQ tests, projectors, VCRs, computers and interviews are just some tools of the trade used in defining a prospect's size, speed, skills, intelligence, potential problems, medical history, maturity and the like.

The most noteworthy pick in the draft each year is the "first first," the player taken with the very first pick in the first round of the draft.

The initial NFL draft took place on February 8, 1936, with running back Jay Berwanger of the University of Chicago being chosen with the first pick by the Philadelphia Eagles. Great names such as Tom Harmon of Michigan, Angelo Bertelli of Notre Dame, Chuck Bednarik of Pennsylvania, Paul Hornung of Notre Dame, Ernie Davis of Syracuse, Tommy Nobis of Texas, O. J. Simpson of Southern California, Terry Bradshaw of Louisiana Tech, Bruce Smith of Virginia Tech, John Elway of Stanford, Troy Aikman of UCLA and Drew Bledsoe of Washington State were first firsts over the years. Quarterback Peyton Manning from the University of Tennessee was the most recent first first, drafted by Indianapolis on April 18, 1998.

The Raiders had only one top first pick in the draft, back on December 2, 1961, when they chose quarterback Roman Gabriel from North Carolina State but were unable to sign him. Eight great athletes who were taken with that pick have played for the Raiders in Oakland and/or Los Angeles, with three on the most recent active roster:

Billy Cannon

Bubba Smith

Jim Plunkett

John Matuszak

Aundray Bruce

Jeff George

Bo Jackson

Russell Maryland

FIRST FIRSTS WITH THE RAIDERS

Player	Pos.	College	Draft	Drafted By	Raider Years
Billy Cannon	RB	Louisiana State	11-22-59	L.A. Rams	1964-69
Bubba Smith	DE	Michigan State	3-14-67	Baltimore	1973-74
Jim Plunkett	QB	Stanford	1-28-71	New England	1978-86
John Matuszak	DE	Tampa	1-30-73	Houston	1976-82
Bo Jackson	RB	Auburn	4-29-86	Tampa Bay	1987-90
Aundray Bruce	LB	Auburn	4-24-88	Atlanta	1992-
Jeff George	QB	Illinois	4-22-90	Indianapolis	1997-
Russell Maryland	DT	Miami	4-21-91	Dallas	1996-

Most of the glamour in the annual college player draft surrounds the picks made in the very first round. These are the big name players featured in the pre-draft articles and publications. Then public interest wanes as the draft proceeds and the rounds roll on.

The highly respected Raiders personnel department never joins that group whose concentration fades as the draft moves forward, no, indeed! Raider finds in the late rounds are legendary for the four decades the organization has been headed by Al Davis.

Running back Marv Hubbard, for instance, was a Raider 11th round choice out of Colgate University in the 1968 draft. Running back Don Highsmith was a 13th round pick out of Michigan State in '70. Defensive end Horace Jones of Louisville was chosen in round 12 in 1971. Outstanding outside linebacker Rod Martin from Southern Cal was a 12th round selection in 1977, while mammoth offensive tackle Bruce Davis of UCLA was an 11th round choice in '79. And defensive lineman Reggie Kinlaw from the University of Oklahoma was a 12th round choice in that same draft.

Three Raider tenth round picks stand out in the '80s: running back Frank Hawkins of Nevada-Reno in 1981; wide receiver Mervyn Fernadez of San Jose State in 1983 and guard John Gesek of Cal State-Sacramento in 1987. Then, in 1991, the Raiders picked tight end Andrew Glover from Grambling in the tenth round. The NFL draft now only goes seven rounds so these double-digit choices can no longer happen.

But round seven has been a very successful source of quality talent for the Silver and Black. Way back in 1967, the Raiders used that round of the draft to select defensive back George Atkinson from little Morris Brown College in Atlanta, Georgia. Atkinson went on to play for 10 seasons and still ranks tenth among all-time Raider pass interceptors, fourth in all-time punt returners and fourth in all-time kickoff returners. In 1972, the Raiders seventh round draft choice was Alonzo "Skip" Thomas from Southern Cal who finished his seven-season career as number 16 in pass interceptions. Both Atkinson and Thomas were starters as the Raiders

Skip Thomas

won the first of their three World Championships of Professional Football in the Super Bowl XI rout of the Minnesota Vikings after the 1976 season.

Seventh round pick Malcolm Barnwell in 1980, a speedy wide receiver out of Virginia Union University in Richmond, Virginia went on to catch 112 passes for 1,941 yards during four seasons of play.

Defensive tackle Mitch Willis of Southern Methodist and center Bill Lewis of Nebraska

George Atkinson

Greg Biekert

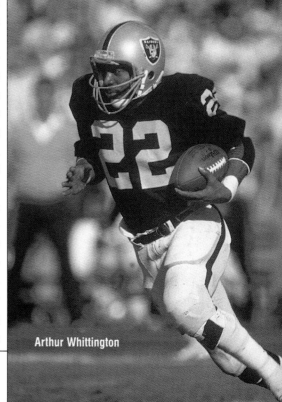

Arthur Whittington

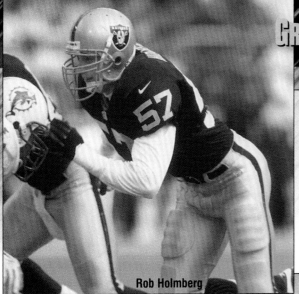

Rob Holmberg

run of over 90 yards, with 92-yard and 91-yard bursts to his credit, along with an 88-yard run. Bo also caught 40 passes for another 372 yards and had eight 100-yards rushing games. He was a Pro Bowl choice in 1990.

The Raiders seventh round draft success continued into the '90s, with linebacker Greg Biekert of Colorado in 1993 and linebacker Rob Holmberg of Penn State in 1994. Biekert is the starting middle linebacker while Holmberg sees action on the outside and is a top special teams performer.

Some people roll the dice looking hopefully for a lucky seven. The Oakland Raiders instead do their homework to find gems in round seven of the college player draft each year.

were seventh rounders in 1984 and 1986 respectively. Lewis was chosen Raider Offensive Lineman of the Year by his teamates in 1988.

Then, in 1987, Al Davis made one of the greatest seventh round picks in NFL history, choosing running back Bo Jackson of Auburn University. One year earlier, Bo Jackson had been the very first player taken in the draft when chosen by the Tampa Bay Buccaneers. Bo chose major league baseball instead, and after one year, his name went back into the NFL Draft. No other organization in the league was willing to compete with baseball for his services but the Raiders, who developed a two-sport participation program with Bo. During the four partial seasons he wore the Silver and Black, before a career-ending hip injury brought his football efforts to a regretable halt, Bo Jackson rushed for 2,782 yards and a Raider-record 5.4 yards per carry. He is the only running back in NFL history to have more than one

Bo Jackson

Mitch Willis

BEST BUY and **Canon**

Always A Winning Combination!
professional tools with a personal touch

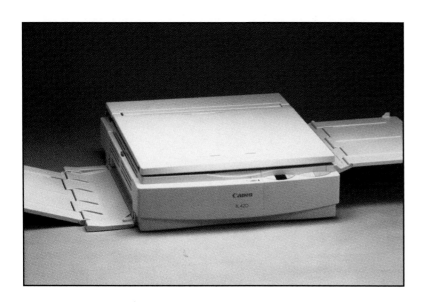

PC420

For home office or personal use, offering portability and multiple copying capability, up to 50 letter-size copies.

- Single Cartridge System for virtually maintenance-free performance
- Starter cartridge included
- 4 copies per minute (letter)
- 50-sheet stack tray accepts postcard to letter-size paper
- Makes up to 50 copies at a time
- Instant warm up; no waiting
- Auto shut-off; saves energy
- Warranty – 1-year overnight exchange

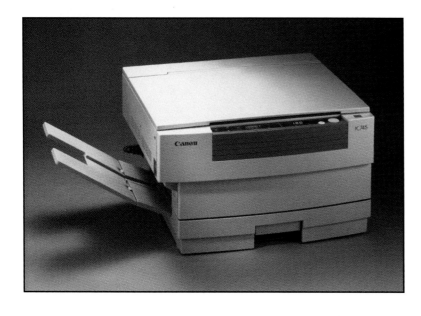

PC 745

Affordable copying for the small office providing zoom features, front-loading paper cassette, and no warm-up time.

- Single Cartridge System for virtually maintenance-free performance – cartridge included
- 10 copies per minute (letter); 9 copies per minute (legal)
- Zoom Reduction & Enlargement from 70% to 141% in 1% increments, & four preset ratios
- 250-sheet front-loading paper cassette accepts statement, letter & legal size paper
- Instant warm up; no waiting
- Makes up to 100 copies at a time
- 3-year warranty - first year on-site

Always Score a Touchdown with Canon Copiers and

The most prominent tradition in the four-decade history of the Raiders is winning, winning on a consistent basis. Incredible comebacks, domination of Monday Night Football, success on the road, conquest of interconference opponents—all traditions of the Raiders.

Great players, great coaches, great plays and great games—more enviable traditions of the Silver and Black.

The offensive center position—that, too, has become a very special tradition of the Raiders. The center—first man out of the offensive huddle, the big man who squats uncomfortably, bent over the football, then scans from side to side to check defensive alignments and makes key "calls" to his linemates to adjust their assignments. The center—a man who snaps the ball to his quarterback to start every offensive play, with no mistakes allowed. He gets every play underway and then must block a big, strong, nasty defender on every one of those plays.

With just a very few exceptions, only five players have handled that challenging position in league and postseason play for the Raiders. Just five very special warriors in 38 seasons in the American Football League and National Football League. Just five men in nearly 600 games from 1960 thru 1997.

Pro Football Hall of Fame member Jim Otto, from the University of Miami, played at center for the Oakland Raiders for 210 consecutive league games—starting every single one. Then Dave Dalby, from UCLA, played in 205 consecutive league games—almost all of them at center. Next, Don Mosebar from the University of Southern California, played in 173 league games, mostly at the center spot. When an unfortunate eye injury suddenly ended Mosebar's streak, Dan Turk of the University of Wisconsin, moved in at center for the 1995 season before giving way to Barret Robbins from Texas Christian University in 1996.

Along with their physical play and football knowledge, centers have to provide emotional strength and stability. Reliability is a key factor. Knowing that a solid, steadying influence is anchored in the middle of the offense, that the same guy is reading the defensive fronts and making the line calls game after game, that continuity is assured—this is comforting to players and coaches alike.

It has become the accepted—and expected—way of the Raiders for a center to help train his eventual replacement since Jim Otto worked overtime to prepare Dave Dalby to step in for him and Dalby did the same to help convert Don Mosebar from tackle to center.

It has also become the Raider way to put the name of your starting center on the lineup sheet at the start of the season and leave it there. These five regulars at center have been durable, tough men who play with aches and pains. Today's fire-breathing nose tackles, lined up just inches away from the center, are mean, nasty, massive 300-pounders, triggered to explode on the very first movement by the center. Then the war begins with helmets clanging, face masks intertwined, shoulder pads slamming. Head, shoulders, hands, midsections, legs, feet— every body part is involved in this physical combat. Toughness, explosiveness, strength, quickness, agility, intensity and intelligence all combine with technique to get the job done.

It is truly amazing in today's era of specialization, frequent injuries, "situation substitution" and the like, that the Raiders have had only five players line up regularly at the center position. But such outstanding players and the meaningful traditions they have helped establish and maintain are among the most important reasons for the four-decade greatness of the Raiders. ◄

Jim Otto

Dave Dalby

Dan Turk

Don Mosebar

Barret Robbins

Fred Biletnikoff and Cliff Branch share strategy on the sidelines in a 1975 game.

Three great Raider wide receivers—Fred Biletnikoff, Cliff Branch and Tim Brown—share a lot more than the same letter at the start of their last name. Each of the superbly talented, extremely competitive pass catchers has more than 500 receptions to his credt. Each gained more than 8,500 yards with those pass receptions. Each scored at least 60 touchdowns on pass receptions. Each played in at least four Pro Bowls. Each was drafted by the Raiders. Each played at least ten years with the Raiders. And each has worn only the Silver and Black in their decades in the National Football League.

Fred Biletnikoff was the Raiders second-round draft choice in 1965 after finishing an outstanding college career as a wide receiver at Florida State University. He played for the Raiders from 1965 thru 1978, catching 589 passes in league games, good for 8,974 yards, 76 touchdowns and an average of 15.2 yards per reception. He played in four AFC-NFC Pro Bowls and two AFL All-Star Games. He is now the Raiders wide receivers coach.

Cliff Branch was a Raider fourth-round draft choice in 1972 after an outstanding college career as a wide receiver, punt returner and occasional running back at the University of Colorado. He played for the Raiders from 1974 thru 1985, catching 501 passes in league games, good for 8,685 yards, 67 touchdowns and an average of 17.3 yards per reception. He played in four AFC-NFC Pro Bowls.

Tim Brown was the Raiders early first-round draft choice in 1988 after an outstanding college career as a wide receiver, return man and

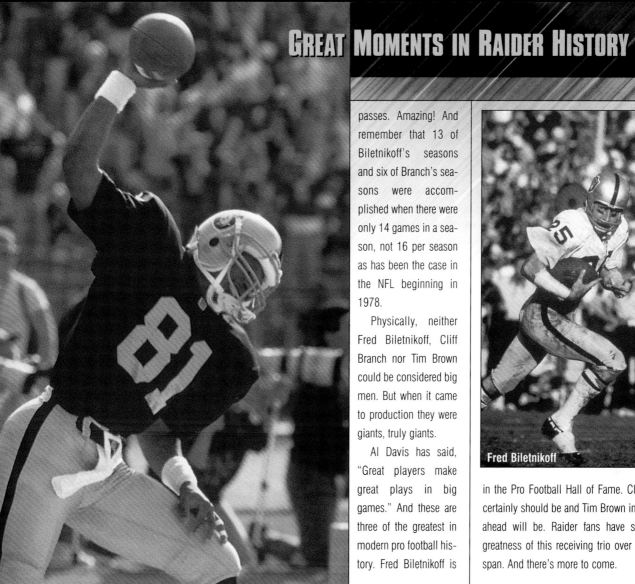

passes. Amazing! And remember that 13 of Biletnikoff's seasons and six of Branch's seasons were accomplished when there were only 14 games in a season, not 16 per season as has been the case in the NFL beginning in 1978.

Physically, neither Fred Biletnikoff, Cliff Branch nor Tim Brown could be considered big men. But when it came to production they were giants, truly giants.

Al Davis has said, "Great players make great plays in big games." And these are three of the greatest in modern pro football history. Fred Biletnikoff is

Fred Biletnikoff

in the Pro Football Hall of Fame. Cliff Branch certainly should be and Tim Brown in the years ahead will be. Raider fans have shared the greatness of this receiving trio over a 33-year span. And there's more to come.

Tim Brown

TOP THREE RAIDER PASS RECEIVERS 1960-1997

Player	Receptions	Yards	Touchdowns	Yards Per Catch
BROWN, TIM	599	8,588	60	14.3
BILETNIKOFF, FRED	589	8,974	76	15.2
BRANCH, CLIFF	501	8,685	67	17.3

occasional running back at the University of Notre Dame. After his senior season at Notre Dame, he was awarded the Heisman Trophy as the outstanding player in college football. He has played with the Raiders since 1988, catching a club-record 599 passes thru 1997, good for 8,588 yards, 60 touchdowns and an average of 14.3 yards per reception. To date he has played in seven Pro Bowls.

The total statistics for these three pass receiving wizards are truly awesome. As a trio they total 1,689 pass receptions for a total of 26,247 yards. That's 14.9 miles gained on pass receptions by Biletnikoff, Branch and Brown. Between them they have caught 203 touchdown

Cliff Branch

The precision passing game—peopled by highly accurate quarterbacks teamed with gifted, sure-handed receivers, operating behind huge offensive lines—this has become the trademark of professional football in the modern era.

No longer is a fifty percent completion the mark of a top passer the the NFL. The average QB in the league in 1997 hit on 56.2 percent of his throws. In '97, there were 617 touchdown passes thrown versus 479 interceptions. Nearly 62 percent of the 1,001 offensive touchdowns scored came thru the air. Yards gained passing per team per game topped 200 yards, at 201.8 yards to be exact.

Defensive coordinators over the decades have tried everything to curtail the aerial attacks they face every weekend throughout the National Football League. Zone defenses, man-to-man defenses, combination defense, blitzes, dogs, stunts, zone blitzes—everything but the kitchen sink has been tried to slow down, if not stop, the continuing, creative passing schemes that

Willie Brown

Lester Hayes

Terry McDaniel

evolve and develop.

A primary means of meeting fire with fire in the Raider pass defense philosophy since Al Davis took over as head coach and general manager in 1963, is to combat the talented passing personnel with great athletes in the defensive secondary. Matchups—speed,

TOP 15 RAIDER CAREER PASS INTERCEPTION LEADERS

Rank	Player	Interceptions	Yards	TDs	Longest
1.	Willie Brown	39	277	2	31
1.	Lester Hayes	39	572	4	62
3.	Terry McDaniel	34	624	5	67
4.	Vann McElroy	31	296	1	35
5.	George Atkinson	30	488	2	41
5.	Jack Tatum	30	636	0	66
7.	Dave Grayson	29	624	4	79
8.	Fred Williamson	25	293	1	91
9.	Tom Morrow	23	348	0	77
9.	Warren Powers	23	366	2	70
11.	Eddie Anderson	19	529	3	102
11.	Charles Phillips	19	293	1	42
11.	Nemiah Wilson	19	213	0	34
11.	Lionel Washington	19	200	3	44
15.	Mike Haynes	18	295	1	97

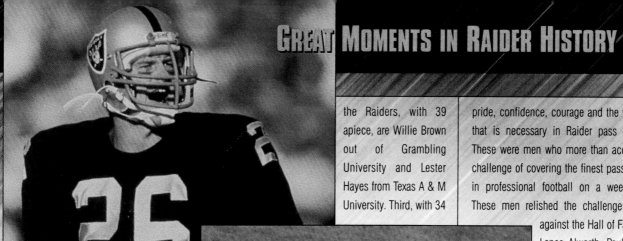

Vann McElroy

the Raiders, with 39 apiece, are Willie Brown out of Grambling University and Lester Hayes from Texas A & M University. Third, with 34

pride, confidence, courage and the will to win that is necessary in Raider pass defenders. These were men who more than accepted the challenge of covering the finest pass receivers in professional football on a weekly basis. These men relished the challenge of going against the Hall of Famers like Lance Alworth, Paul Warfield, Charlie Jones, Mike Ditka, John Mackey, Steve Largent, Don Manyard and Kellen Winslow; against lesser known but highly talented pass catchers and no-name players alike.

These defensive aces respected every opponent every week; prepared for each thoroughly by film study, scouting report review, in practice and on the blackboard. They got ready; they stayed ready; they played ready.

Al Davis has defined great players as "those who make big plays in big games." These interception leaders were great players.

quickness, agility, burst, "athleticism" on the corners and at the safety posts to equal or exceed the similarly gifted attackers on offense.

Turnovers are the bane of existence of any offensive scheme—and nothing is more shattering to a passing game than the hated pass interception.

Throughout the Al Davis decades, the Raiders secondaries have had great athletes to police and battle the high quality receivers sent their way. Two of those superb corners—Willie Brown and Mike Haynes—have already been enshrined in the Pro Football Hall of Fame. Others may have such greatness shine their way in years to come. Many without the hype or statistics to gain such lofty recognition have been blessed with something of equal value— the respect of those they play against and of their teammates.

The top ten pass interceptors in Raider history total 302 pass interceptions among them. That's 302 times that one of these pass defenders in Silver and Black stopped an opponent dead in their tracks, halted a drive, curtailed a march, denied them the end zone, took over the ball, said "No way," The interception leaders for

George Atkinson

thefts, is Terry McDaniel from the University of Tennessee. Fourth is Vann McElroy from Baylor University who picked off 31 passes. Tied for fifth with 30 interceptions are George Atkinson of little Morris Brown College in Atlanta, Georgia and Jack Tatum of giant Ohio State University in Columbus, Ohio.

Brown, Hayes and McDaniel were cornerbacks. McElroy, Atkinson and Tatum were safeties. McDaniel and Tatum were first round draft choices, McElroy was a third round pick, Hayes a fifth rounder, Atkinson a seventh round choice and Brown a free agent.

All six were gifted athletes with personal

Jack Tatum

Ken Stabler passed for 19,078 yards with the Raiders. Fred Biletnikoff gained 8,944 yards on pass receptions with the Raiders. Marcus Allen rushed for 8,545 yards with the Raiders. Bo Roberson gained 2,791 yards on kickoff returns with the Raiders. Tim Brown gained 3,083 yards on punt returns with the Raiders. These five players—each the Raider leader in their statistic totaled 42,471 yards gained in these five categories. Impres-sive numbers, indeed!

Yet there is one great Raider player who by himself moved the ball for two thousand more yards than these five stars combined. That's right. In his 14 years in Silver and Black—1973 thru 1986—Ray Guy punted the ball for 44,541 yards in his 207 league games for the Raiders.

Ray Guy, the first punter ever taken in the first round of the National Football League col-lege player draft when chosen first by the Oak-land Raiders in the 1973 draft, went onto become the finest punter in the game. His num-bers are legendary: A Raider single season average of 45.3 yards per punt in his rookie year of 1973; leading the AFC in punting three times; leading the NFL in punting three times; being chosen to play in the Pro Bowl seven times including six consecutive years from 1973 thru 1978; going 619 punts without hav-ing one blocked; more punts in postseason games than any other punter in NFL history; the best punting average in a playoff game of any punter in NFL history—and the count goes on.

Ray Guy was always a great punter.

"I think I was born to be a punter," he once explained. "I've been punting since I was six years old."

The Georgia native averaged 52 yards per punt at Thomson (Ga.) High School, with some of the yardage on the bounces as a lot of high school return men couldn't field his punts. Guy, who won 16 varsity letters in high school, was also an All-State quarter-back and safety and an outstanding pitcher in baseball. In high school and college he was drafted four times by major league baseball teams.

Guy attended Southern Mississip-pi University where he lettered in both baseball and football. In his three col-lege seasons he intercepted 18 pass-es at the safety spot and led the nation in punting in 1972 as a senior with a 46.2 yard average. That included a 93-yard punt against the University of Mississippi which, according to press clippings, rolled out of the end zone and was finally stopped by a retaining wall. Guy was standing five yards deep in his own end zone when he punted the ball and said it traveled 125 yards.

On January 30, 1973, another great moment in Raider history, the organization used the 23rd pick in

round one to select Ray Guy as its first draft choice.

"To us, Guy stood out," recalls then-Raider head coach John Madden. "It was the easiest, simplest and most unanimous decision we ever made. Some scouts laughed at us at the time, going that high for a specialist. They didn't laugh for long. We knew what he could do."

For both John Madden, who coached Ray Guy from 1973 thru 1978, and Tom Flores, who had him from 1979 thru his retirement after the 1986 season, his booming punts added another dimension to the game plan.

Ray Guy often sacrificed distance on his punts to go for field position to aid the Raider defense. Individual statistics were never his goals. To Ray Guy the statistic that counted was the final score, the wins or losses, not the punting average.

Height and "hang time" were important items in Ray Guy's punting portfolio. When it came to the high ball it should be noted that Guy was the first punter to ever hit the giant television screen pod suspended from the rafters of the Louisiana Superdome.

"The higher I kick it, the longer it stays up in the air and the more time it gives our guys to get down field and cover," Guy explained.

Speaking of height reminds former head coach Tom Flores of another brilliant play his punter made in Super Bowl XVIII against the Washington Redskins in Tampa. Guy leaped high to grab a misfired punt snap, pulled it down and still got a booming kick off.

"People may not remember that so readily because he did it so very effortlessly," recalls Flores. "But what a big play it was. We were leading 7-0 at the time, and if Ray hadn't saved that ball, Washington would have had it inside our 20-yard line."

That was only one of three Super Bowls in which Ray Guy played for the Silver and Black—all wins for the Raiders. During Guy's 14 seasons with

Ray Guy leaps high to save a bad snap and get the punt off in Super Bowl XVIII.

the organization the Raiders had a regular season record of 143-63-1 for a .694 winning percentage.

Classic form with results to match were the norm for Raider punter Ray Guy.

Jerrel Wilson, himself a top punter with the Kansas City Chiefs in those same years as Ray Guy's tenure, said this about the Raider punter, "He's the best. There never has been a punter in the game as good as Ray Guy."

"Ray Guy's probably the best ever at his position in the history of the game," says Tom Flores. "He was clearly the best I've ever seen," added Flores, who has been in professional football since the late 1950's.

"When we first drafted him, it was a heck of a choice," John Madden commented. "I thought then he could be the greatest in the league, but I changed my mind. I think Ray proved he's the best of all-time."

George Atkinson

A

ACKERMAN, Rick	Memphis State	DT	1984, 87
ADAMS, Stanley	Memphis State	LB	1984
ADAMS, Stefon	East Carolina	DB	1986-89
AGAJANIAN, Ben	New Mexico	K	1962
AIKENS, Carl	Northern Illinois	WR	1987
ALEXANDER, Mike	Penn State	WR	1989-90
ALLEN, Dalva	Houston	DE	1962-64
ALLEN, Jackie	Baylor	DB	1969
ALLEN, Marcus	Southern California	RB	1982-92
ALZADO, Lyle	Yankton	DE	1982-85
ANDERSON, Eddie	Fort Valley State	DB	1987-97
ARAGUZ, Leo	Stephen F. Austin	P	1996-97
ARCHER, Dan	Oregon	T	1967
ARMSTRONG, Ramon	Texas Christian	T	1960
ASAD, Doug	Northwestern	TE	1960-61
ASKA, Joe	Central Oklahoma	RB	1995-97
ATKINS, Pervis	New Mexico State	WR	1965-66
ATKINSON, George	Morris Brown	DB	1968-77

Pete Banazak

B

BAHR, Chris	Penn State	K	1980-88
BALDWIN, Keith	Texas A&M	DE	1988
BALL, Eric	UCLA	RB	1995
BALL, Jerry	Southern Methodist	DT	1994-96
BANASZAK, Pete	Miami	RB	1966-78
BANKS, Estes	Colorado	RB	1967
BANKSTON, Warren	Tulane	TE	1973-78
BANSAVAGE, Al	Southern California	LB	1961
BARBEE, Joe	Kent State	T	1960
BARKSDALE, Rod	Arizona	WR	1986
BARNES, Jeff	California	LB	1977-87
BARNES, Larry	Colorado State	LB	1960
BARNES, Rodrigo	Rice	LB	1976
BARNWELL, Malcolm	Virginia Union	WR	1981-84
BARRETT, Jan	Fresno State	TE	1963-64
BATES, Patrick	Texas A&M	DB	1993-94
BELCHER, Kevin	Wisconsin	T	1985
BELL, Anthony	Michigan State	LB	1992
BELL, Greg	Notre Dame	RB	1990
BELL, Joe	Norfolk State	DE	1979

BELL, Nick	Iowa	RB	1991-93
BENDER, Wes	Southern California	RB	1994
BENSON, Duane	Hamline	LB	1967-71
BENSON, Tom	Oklahoma	LB	1989-91
BERNS, Rick	Nebraska	RB	1982-83
BESS, Rufus	South Carolina State	DB	1979
BESSILLIEU, Don	Georgia Tech	DB	1983, 85
BEUERLEIN, Steve	Notre Dame	QB	1988-90
BIEKERT, Greg	Colorado	LB	1993-97
BILETNIKOFF, Fred	Florida State	WR	1965-78
BIRD, Rodger	Kentucky	DB	1967-71
BIRDWELL, Dan	Houston	DT	1962-69
BISHOP, Sonny	Fresno State	G	1963
BLACK, Barry	Boise State	G	1987
BLANDA, George	Kentucky	QB-K	1967-75
BLANKENSHIP, Greg	Cal State-Hayward	LB	1976
BONNESS, Rik	Nebraska	LB	1976
BOYD, Greg	San Diego State	DT	1984
BOYDSTON, Max	Oklahoma	TE	1962
BOYNTON, George	East Texas State	DB	1962
BRABHAM, Cary	Southern Methodist	DB	1994
BRACELIN, Greg	California	LB	1981
BRADSHAW, Morris	Ohio State	WR	1974-81
BRANCH, Calvin	Colorado State	DB	1997
BRANCH, Cliff	Colorado	WR	1972-85
BRANTON, Gene	Texas Southern	TE	1987
BRAVO, Alex	California Poly, SLO	DB	1960-61
BREECH, Jim	California	K	1976-79
BREWINGTON, Jim	North Carolina College	T	1961
BROUGHTON, Willie	Miami	DT	1992-94
BROWN, Bob	Nebraska	T	1971-73
BROWN, Charles	Houston	T	1962
BROWN, Doug	Fresno State	DT	1964
BROWN, Larry	Texas Christian	DB	1996-97
BROWN, Ron	Southern California	DE	1987-88
BROWN, Ron	Arizona State	DB	1990
BROWN, Tim	Notre Dame	WR	1988-97
BROWN, Willie	Grambling	DB	1967-78
BROWNE, Jim	Boston College	RB	1987
BROWNER, Keith	Southern California	LB	1987
BROWNING, Dave	Washington	DE-DT	1978-82
BRUCE, Aundray	Auburn	DE	1992-97
BRUNSON, Larry	Colorado	WR	1978-79
BUCZKOWSKI, Bob	Pittsburgh	DE	1987
BUDNESS, Bill	Boston University	LB	1964-70
BUEHLER, George	Stanford	G	1969-78
BUIE, Drew	Catawba	WR	1969-71
BURCH, Gerald	Georgia Tech	TE	1961
BURTON, Ron	North Carolina	LB	1990
BUTCHER, Paul	Wayne State	LB	1996
BRYANT, Warren	Kentucky	T	1984
BYRD, Darryl	Illinois	LB	1983-84, 87

Raymond Chester

C

CALDWELL, Tony	Washington	LB	1983-85

CALHOUN, Rick	Cal State-Fullerton	RB	1987
CAMARILLO, Rich	Washington	P	1996
CAMPBELL, Joe	Maryland	DE	1980-81
CAMPBELL, Stan	Iowa State	G	1962
CANNAVINO, Joe	Ohio State	DB	1960-61
CANNON, Billy	Louisiana State	TE	1964-69
CARR, Chetti	Northwest Oklahoma	WR	1987
CARRINGTON, Darren	Northern Arizona	S	1996
CARROLL, Joe	Pittsburgh	LB	1972-73
CARTER, Louis	Maryland	RB	1975
CARTER, Perry	Mississippi	CB	1996-97
CARTER, Russell	Southern Methodist	DB	1988-89
CASH, Kerry	Texas	TE	1995
CASPER, Dave	Notre Dame	TE	1974-80, 84
CAVALLI, Carmen	Richmond	DE	1960
CELOTTO, Mario	Southern California	LB	1980-81
CHANDLER, Bob	Southern California	WR	1980-82
CHAPMAN, Ted	Maryland	DE	1987
CHARLES, Mike	Syracuse	DT	1990
CHESTER, Raymond	Morgan State	TE	1970-72, 78-81
CHRISTENSEN, Todd	Brigham Young	RB-TE	1979-88
CHURCHWELL, Hansen	Mississippi	DT	1960
CLAY, John	Missouri	T	1987
CLINE, Tony	Miami	DE	1970-75
COLZIE, Neal	Ohio State	DB	1975-78
COLLONS, Ferric	California	DT	1993
CONNERS, Dan	Miami	LB	1964-74
COOLBAUGH, Bob	Richmond	WR	1961
COOPER, Earl	Rice	TE	1986
CORMIER, Joe	Southern California	LB	1987
COSTA, Dave	Utah	DT	1963-65
COSTELLO, Joe	Central Connecticut	LB	1989
CRAIG, Dobie	Howard Payne	WR	1962-63
CRAIG, Roger	Nebraska	RB	1991
CROW, Wayne	California	RB-DB	1960-61
CRUDUP, Derrick	Oklahoma	DB	1989,1991
CUNNINGHAM, Rick	Texas A&M	T	1996-97

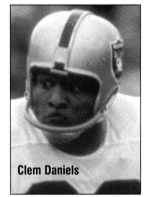

Clem Daniels

D

DALBY, Dave	UCLA	C-G	1972-85
DANIELS, Clemon	Prairie View	RB	1961-67
DANIELS, David	Florida A&M	DT	1966
DAVIDSON, Ben	Washington	DE	1964-71
DAVIDSON, Cotton	Baylor	QB	1962-69
DAVIS, Bruce	UCLA	T	1979-87
DAVIS, Clarence	Southern California	RB	1971-78
DAVIS, James	Southern	DB	1982-87
DAVIS, Mike	Colorado	DB	1978-85
DAVIS, Scott	Illinois	DE	1988-91,94
DAVISON, Jerone	Arizona State	RB	1996-97
DENNERY, Mike	Southern Mississippi	LB	1974-75
DePOYSTER, Jerry	Wyoming	K	1971-72

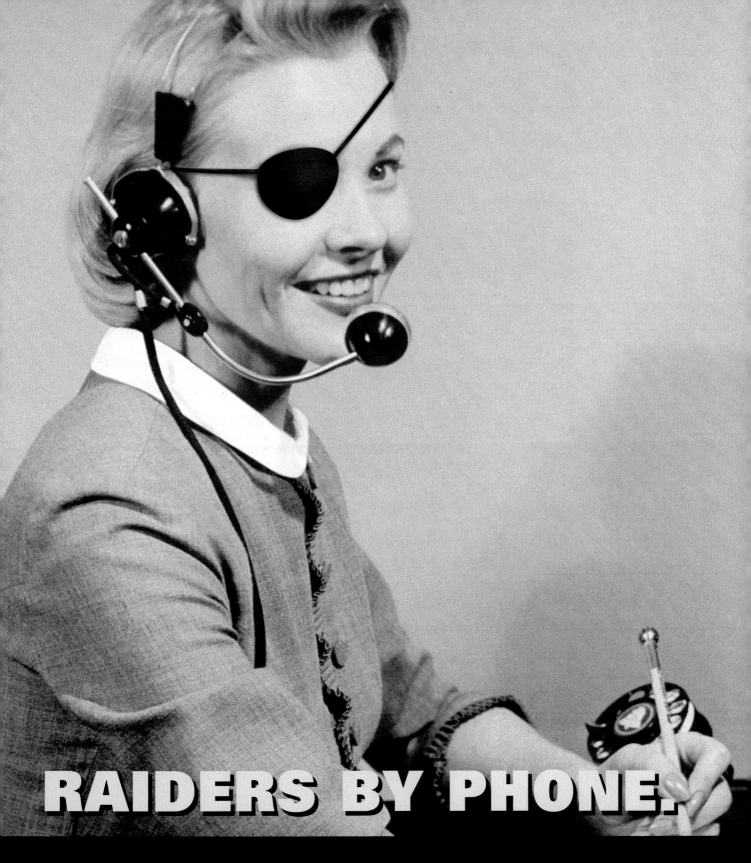

RAIDERS BY PHONE.

DESKINS, Don	Michigan	G	1960
DICKERSON, Andy	California Lutheran	G	1987
DICKERSON, Eric	Southern Methodist	RB	1992
DICKEY, Eldridge	Tennessee State	WR	1968-71
DICKINSON, Bo	Southern Mississippi	RB	1964
DIEHL, John	Virginia	DT	1965
DITTRICH, John	Wisconsin	G	1960
DIXON, Hewritt	Florida A&M	RB	1966-70
DIXON, Rickey	Oklahoma	DB	1993
DORN, Torin	North Carolina	DB	1990-93
DORSEY, Dick	Southern California	WR	1962
DOTSON, Al	Grambling	DT	1968-70
DOUGHERTY, Bob	Kentucky	LB	1960-63
DUDLEY, Rickey	Ohio State	TE	1996-97
DUFAULT, Paul	New Hampshire	C-G	1987
DUFF, John	New Mexico	TE-DE	1993-94
DYAL, Mike	Texas A&I	TE	1989-90
DYSON, Matt	Michigan	DT/LB	1995

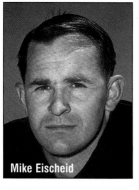

Mike Eischeid

EASON, John	Florida A&M	TE	1968
EDMONDS, Bobby Joe	Arkansas	WR	1989
EDWARDS, Lloyd	San Diego State	TE	1969
EISCHEID, Mike	Upper Iowa	K	1966-71
ELLIS, Craig	San Diego State	RB	1987
ELLIS, Jim	Boise State	LB	1987
ELLISON, Glenn	Arkansas	RB	1971
ELLISON, Riki	Southern California	LB	1990-92
ENIS, Hunter	Texas Christian	QB	1962
ENYART, Bill	Oregon State	LB	1971
EVANS, Vince	Southern California	QB	1987-95

fMervyn Fernandez

FAIRBAND, Bill	Colorado	LB	1967-68
FELLOWS, Ron	Missouri	DB	1987-88
FENNER, Derrick	North Carolina	RB	1996-97
FERNANDEZ, Mervyn	San Jose State	WR	1987-92
FICCA, Dan	Southern California	G	1982
FIELDS, George	Bakersfield J.C.	DT	1960-61
FINNERAN, Garry	Southern California	DT	1961
FITZPATRICK, James	Southern California	G-T	1990-91

FLEMING, George	Washington	RB	1961
FLORES, Tom	Pacific	QB	1960-61, 63-66
FOLSTON, James	Northeast Louisiana	LB	1994-97
FORD, Cole	Southern California	K	1995-97
FOSTER, Ron	Cal State-Northridge	DB	1987
FRANKLIN, Keith	South Carolina	LB	1995
FRANK, Donald	Winston-Salem	DB	1994
FRANKS, Elvis	Morgan State	DE	1985-86
FREDRICKSON, Rob	Michigan State	LB	1994-97
FREEMAN, Mike	Arizona	G	1988
FREEMAN, Russell	Georgia Tech	T	1995
FULCHER, David	Arizona State	LB	1993
FULLER, Charles	San Francisco State	RB	1961-62

Ray Guy

GALLEGOS, Chon	San Jose State	QB	1962
GAMACHE, Vince	Cal State-Northridge	K	1987
GARNER, Bob	Fresno State	DB	1961-62
GARRETT, Carl	New Mexico Highlands	RB	1976-77
GAULT, Willie	Tennessee	WR	1988-93
GEORGE, Jeff	Illinois	QB	1997
GESEK, John	Sacramento State	G	1987-89
GIBSON, Claude	North Carolina State	DB	1963-65
GILLETT, Fred	Los Angeles State	TE	1964
GINN, Hubie	Florida A&M	RB	1976-78
GIPSON, Tom	North Texas State	DT	1971
GLOVER, Andrew	Grambling	TE	1991-96
GLOVER, La'Roi	San Diego State	DT	1996
GOGAN, Kevin	Washington	G	1994-96
GOLDSTEIN, Alan	North Carolina	WR	1960
GOLIC, Bob	Notre Dame	DT	1989-92
GOLSTEYN, Jerry	Northern Illinois	QB	1984
GOLTZ, Rick	Simon Fraser	DE	1987
GOODLOW, Darryl	Oklahoma	LB	1987
GORDON, Alex	Cincinnati	LB	1990
GOSSETT, Jeff	Eastern Illinois	P	1988-96
GRADDY, Sam	Tennessee	WR	1990-92
GRAHAM, Jeff	Long Beach State	QB	1995
GRAVES, Rory	Ohio State	T	1988-91
GRAYSON, David	Oregon	DB	1965-70
GREEN, Charley	Wittenberg	QB	1966
GREENWOOD, David	Wisconsin	DB	1988
GRIMES, Phil	Central Missouri	DE	1987
GROSSART, Kyle	Oregon State	QB	1980
GUY, Louie	Mississippi	DB	1984
GUY, Ray	Southern Mississippi	K	1973-86

Marv Hubbard

H

HAGBERG, Roger	Minnesota	RB	1965-69
HALL, Tim	Robert Morris	RB	1996-97
HALL, Willie	Southern California	LB	1975-78
HANNAH, Charley	Alabama	G	1983-88
HARDEN, Mike	Michigan	DB	1989-90
HARDMAN, Cedrick	North Texas State	DE	1980-81
HARDY, Charles	San Jose State	WR	1960-62
HARDY, David	Texas A&M	K	1987
HARKEY, Lance	Illinois	DB	1987
HARLOW, Pat	Southern California	T	1996-97
HARRIS, John	Santa Monica J.C.	DB	1960-61
HARRISON, Dwight	Texas A&I	DB	1960
HARRISON, Nolan	Indiana	DT-DE	1991-96
HARRISON, Rob	Cal State-Sacramento	RB	1987
HART, Harold	Texas Southern	RB	1974-75, 78
HART, Roy	South Carolina	DT	
HARVEY, James	Mississippi	G	1966-71
HASSELBECK, Don	Colorado	TE	1983
HAWKINS, Clarence	Florida A&M	RB	1979
HAWKINS, Frank	Nevada, Reno	RB	1981-87
HAWKINS, Mike	Texas A&I	LB	1982
HAWKINS, Wayne	Pacific	G	1960-70
HAYES, Lester	Texas A&M	DB	1977-86
HAYNES, Mike	Arizona State	DB	1983-89
HEINRICH, Don	Washington	QB	1962
HENDRICKS, Ted	Miami	LB	1975-83
HERMANN, Dick	Florida State	LB	1985
HEROCK, Ken	West Virginia	TE	1963-65, 67
HESTER, Jessie	Florida State	WR	1985-87
HIGHSMITH, Don	Michigan State	RB	1970-72
HILGER, Rusty	Oklahoma State	QB	1985-87
HILL, Greg	Oklahoma State	DB	1987
HILL, Kenny	Yale	DB	1981-83
HILL, Rod	Kentucky State	DB	1987
HINTON, Marcus	Alcorn State	TE	1995-96
HIPP, I.M.	Nebraska	RB	1980
HOBBS, Daryl	Pacific	WR	1993-96
HOBERT, Billy Joe	Washington	QB	1993-96
HOISINGTON, Al	Pasadena J.C.	WR	1960
HOLLAND, Jamie	Ohio State	WR	1990-91
HOLLAS, Donald	Rice	QB	1997
HOLLOWAY, Brian	Stanford	G-T	1987-88
HOLMBERG, Rob	Penn State	LB	1994-97
HOLMES, Lester	Jackson State	G	1997
HOPKINS, Jerry	Texas A&M	LB	1968
HORTON, Ethan	North Carolina	RB-TE	1987, 1989-93
HOSKINS, Derrick	Southern Mississippi	S	1992-95
HOSTETLER, Jeff	West Virginia	QB	1993-96
HOWARD, Desmond	Michigan	WR	1997
HUBBARD, Marv	Colgate	RB	1969-75
HUDSON, Bob	Northeast Oklahoma	RB	1973-74
HUDDLESTON, John	Utah	LB	1978-79
HUMM, David	Nebraska	QB	1975-79, 83-84
HUNLEY, Ricky	Arizona	LB	1989-90

Gerald Irons

I

IRONS, Gerald	Maryland State	LB	1970-75
ISMAIL, Raghib	Notre Dame	WR	1993-95

Bo Jackson

J

JACKSON Bo	Auburn	RB	1987-90
JACKSON Bobby	New Mexico State	RB	1964
JACKSON, Grady	Knoxville	DT	1997
JACKSON, Leonard	Oklahoma State	LB	1987
JACKSON, Monte	San Diego State	DB	1978-82
JACKSON, Richard	Southern	LB	1966
JACKSON, Steve	Louisiana State	DB	1977
JACKSON, Victor	Bowie State	DB	1987
JACOBS, Proverb	California	T	1963-64
JAEGER, Jeff	Washington	K	1989-95
JAGIELSKI, Harry	Indiana	DT	1961
JAKOWENKO, George	Syracuse	K	1974
JELACIC, Jon	Minnesota	DE	1961-64
JENKINS, Robert	UCLA	T	1994-96
JENNINGS, Rick	Maryland	WR	1976-77
JENSEN, Derrick	Texas Arlington	RB-TE	1979-86
JENSEN, Russ	California Lutheran	QB	1985
JETT, James	West Virginia	WR	1993-97
JIMERSON, A.J.	Norfolk State	LB-DE	1990-91
JOHNSON, Kevin	Texas Southern	DT	1997
JOHNSON, Monte	Nebraska	LB	1973-80
JOHNSTONE, Lance	Temple	DE	1996-97
JONES, Calvin	Nebraska	RB	1994-95
JONES, David	Delaware State	TE	1992
JONES, Horace	Louisville	DE	1971-75
JONES, Jim	Washington	LB	1961
JONES, Mike	Missouri	LB	1991-96
JONES, Sean	Northeastern	DE	1984-87
JONES, Willie	Florida State	DE	1979-82
JORDAN, Charles	Long Beach City Col.	WR	1993
JORDAN, Shelby	Washington (MO.)	T	1983-86
JORDAN, Randy	North Carolina	RB	1993
JOYNER, L.C.	Diablo Valley J.C.	DB	1960
JUNKIN, Trey	Louisiana Tech	TE	1985-89, 96

Kenny King

K

KAUFMAN, Napoleon	Washington	RB	1995-97
KEATING, Tom	Michigan	DT	1966-72
KELLY, Joe	Washington	LB	1993
KENNEDY, Lincoln	Washington	T	1996-97
KENT, Greg	Utah	T	1966
KEYES, Bob	San Diego	RB	1960
KIDD, Carl	Arkansas	DB	1995-96
KIMMEL, Jamie	Syracuse	LB	1986-88
KING, Emanuel	Alabama	LB	1989
KING, Joe	Oklahoma State	DB	1995
KING, Kenny	Oklahoma	RB	1980-85
KING, Linden	Colorado State	LB	1986-89
KINLAW, Reggie	Oklahoma	DT	1979-84
KLEIN, Dick	Iowa	T	1963-64
KLINGER, David	Houston	QB	1996-97
KOCH, Pete	Maryland	DE	1989
KOCOUREK, Dave	Wisconsin	TE	1967-68
KOEGEL, Warren	Penn State	C	1971
KOHN, Tim	Iowa State	G	1997
KORVER, Kelvin	Northwestern (Iowa)	DT	1973-77
KOWALCZYK, Walt	Michigan State	RB	1961
KOY, Ted	Texas	TE	1970
KRAKOSKI, Joe	Illinois	DB	1963-66
KRUSE, Bob	Wayne State	G	1967-68
KUNZ, Terry	Colorado	RB	1976-77
KWALICK, Ted	Penn State	TE	1975-77
KYSAR, Jeff	Arizona State	T	1995-96

Daryle Lamonica

L

LACHEY, Jim	Ohio State	T	1988
LAMONICA, Daryle	Notre Dame	QB	1967-74
LAND, Dan	Albany State	DB	1989-97
LANIER, Ken	Florida State	T	1993
LARSCHIED, Jack	Pacific	RB	1960-61
LARSON, Paul	California	QB	1960
LASKEY, Bill	Michigan	LB	1966-70
LASSITER, Issac	St. Augustine	DE	1965-69
LATHAN, Greg	Cincinnati	WR	1987
LAWRENCE, Henry	Florida A&M	T	1974-86
LAWRENCE, Larry	Iowa	QB	1974-75

LEE, Zeph	Southern California	RB-DB	1987-89
LEVITT, Chad	Cornell	RB	1997
LEWIS, Albert	Grambling	DB	1994-97
LEWIS, Bill	Nebraska	C-G	1986-89
LEWIS, Garry	Alcorn State	DB	1990-91
LEWIS, Harold	Houston	RB	1962
LEWIS, Tahaun	Nebraska	DB	1991
LILES, Alva	Boise State	DT	1980
LLOYD, Doug	North Dakota State	RB	1991
LOCKETT, Wade	Cal State-Fullerton	WR	1987
LOCKLIN, Billy Ray	New Mexico State	G	1960
LOFTON, James	Stanford	WR	1987-88
LONG, Howie	Villanova	DE-DT	1981-93
LOTT, Billy	Mississippi	RB	1960
LOTT, Ronnie	Southern California	DB	1991-92
LOUDERBACK, Tom	San Jose State	LB	1960-61
LYNCH, Lorenzo	Sacramento State	S	1996-97
LYONS, Lamar	Washington	S	1996

Matt Millen

M

MACON, Ed	Pacific	DB	1960
MacKINNON, Jacque	Colgate	TE	1970
MANN, Errol	North Dakota	K	1976-78
MANOUKIAN, Don	Stanford	G	1960
MARINOVICH, Marv	Southern California	G	1965
MARINOVICH, Todd	Southern California	QB	1991-92
MARSH, Curt	Washington	G	1981-86
MARTIN, Rod	Southern California	LB	1977-88
MARTINI, Rich	California-Davis	WR	1979-80
MARVIN, Mickey	Tennessee	G	1977-87
MARYLAND, Russell	Miami	DT	1996-97
MASON, Lindsey	Kansas	T	1978-81
MATSOS, Arch	Michigan State	LB	1963-65
MATTHEWS, Ira	Wisconsin	RB-WR	1979-81
MATUSZAK, John	Tampa	DE-DT	1976-82
MAXWELL, Tom	Texas A&M	DB	1971-73
MAYBERRY, Doug	Utah State	RB	1963
McCALL, Joe	Pittsburgh	RB	1984
McCALLUM, Napoleon	U.S. Naval Academy	RB	1986, 1990-94
McCLANAHAN, Randy	Southwestern Louisiana	LB	1977, 80-82
McCLOUGHAN, Kent	Nebraska	DB	1965-70
McCOLL, Milt	Stanford	LB	1988
McCOY, Larry	Lamar	LB	1984
McCOY, Mike	Notre Dame	DT	1977-78
McDANIEL, Terry	Tennessee	DB	1988-97
McELROY, Reggie	West Texas State	G-T	1991-92
McELROY, Vann	Baylor	DB	1982-87
McFARLAN, Nyle	Brigham Young	DE	1960
McGLOCKTON, Chester	Clemson	DT	1992-97
McKENZIE, Reggie	Tennessee	LB	1985-88
McKINNEY, Odis	Colorado	DB	1980-86
McLEMORE, Chris	Arizona	RB	1987-88
McMATH, Herb	Morningside	DT	1976

All-Time Raiders Players 1960–1997

McMILLEN, Dan	Colorado	LB	1987
McMILLIN, Jim	Colorado State	DB	1963-64
McMURTRY, Chuck	Whittier	DT	1962-63
McRAE, Charles	Tennessee	T	1996
MEDLIN, Dan	North Carolina State	G	1974-76
MENDENHALL, Terry	San Diego State	LB	1971-72
MERCER, Mike	Northern Arizona	K	1963-65
MERRILL, Mark	Minnesota	LB	1984
MILLEN, Matt	Penn State	LB	1980-88
MILLER, Alan	Boston College	RB	1961-63, 65
MILLER, Bill	Miami	WR	1964, 66-68
MILLS, John Henry	Wake Forest	LB-TE	1997
MINGO, Gene	None	K	1964-65
MIRALDI, Dean	Utah	G	1987
MIRICH, Rex	Northern Arizona	DT	1964-66
MISCHAK, Bob	U.S. Military Academy	TE-G	1963-65
MITCHELL, Tom	Bucknell	TE	1966
MIX, Ron	Southern California	T	1971
MOFFETT, Tim	Mississippi	WR	1985-86
MONTALBO, Mel	Utah State	DB	1962
MONTEZ, Alfred	Western New Mexico	QB	1996
MONTGOMERY, Cle	Abilene Christian	RB-WR	1981-85
MONTGOMERY, Tyrone	Mississippi	RB	1993-94
MONTOYA, Max	UCLA	G	1990-94
MOODY, Keith	Syracuse	DB	1980
MOORE, Bob	Stanford	TE	1971-75
MOORE, Manfred	Southern California	RB	1976
MORRIS, Riley	Florida A&M	DE	1960-62
MORRISON, Dave	Southwest Texas State	DB	1968
MORROW, Tom	Southern Mississippi	DB	1962-64
MORTON, Mike	North Carolina	LB	1995-97
MOSEBAR, Don	Southern California	C-G-T	1983-94
MOSS, Winston	Miami	LB	1991-94
MOSTARDI, Rich	Kent State	DB	1962
MRAZ, Mark	Utah State	DE	1989
MUELLER, Vance	Occidental	RB	1986-91
MUHAMMAD, Calvin	Texas Southern	WR	1982-83
MUIRBROOK, Shay	Brigham Young	LB	1997
MURANSKY, Ed	Michigan	G-T	1982-84
MURDOCK, Jesse	California Western	RB	1963
MUSTAFAA, Najee	Georgia Tech	DB	1995

Carleton Oats

O

OATS, Carleton	Florida A&M	DT	1965-72
OGAS, Dave	San Diego State	LB	1968
OGLESBY, Paul	UCLA	T	1960
OLIVER, Ralph	Southern California	LB	1968-69
OSBORNE, Clancy	Arizona State	LB	1963-64
O'STEEN, Dwayne	San Jose State	DB	1980-81
OTTO, Gus	Missouri	LB	1965-72
OTTO, Jim	Miami	C	1960-74
OWENS, Burgess	Miami	DB	1980-82

Jim Plunkett

P

PAPAC, Nick	Fresno State	QB	1961
PARILLI, Babe	Kentucky	QB	1960
PARKER, Andy	Utah	TE	1984-88
PASTORINI, Dan	Santa Clara	QB	1980
PATTEN, Joel	Duke	T	1991
PATTERSON, Elvis	Kansas	DB	1990-93
PATTISON, Mark	Washington	WR	1986
PEAR, Dave	Washington	DT	1979-80
PEAT, Todd	Northern Illinois	G	1990, 1993
PERRY, Gerald	Southern	T	1993-95
PERRY, Mario	Mississippi	TE	1987
PETERS, Volney	Southern California	DT	1961
PETERSON, Calvin	UCLA	LB	1982
PHILLIPS, Charles	Southern California	DB	1975-80
PHILLIPS, Irvin	Arkansas Tech	DB	1983
PHILLIPS, Jess	Michigan State	RB	1975
PHILYAW, Charles	Texas Southern	DE	1976-79
PICKEL, Bill	Rutgers	DT-DE	1983-90
PICKENS, Bruce	Nebraska	DB	1995
PITTS, Frank	Southern	WR	1974
PLUNKETT, Jim	Stanford	QB	1978-86
PORTER, Kerry	Washington State	RB	1989
POWELL, Art	San Jose State	WR	1963-66
POWELL, Charlie	None	DE	1960-61
POWERS, Warren	Nebraska	DB	1963-68
PREBOLA, Gene	Boston University	TE	1960
PRICE, Dennis	UCLA	DB	1988-89
PROUT, Bob	Knox	DB	1974
PRUITT, Greg	Oklahoma	RB	1982-84
PYLE, Palmer	Michigan State	G	1966
PYLES, David	Miami (Ohio)	T	1987
QUEEN, Jeff	Morgan State	RB-TE	1973

Bob Nelson

N

NELSON, Bob	Nebraska	LB	1980-85
NICKLAS, Pete	Baylor	T	1962
NOBLE, Mike	Stanford	LB	1987
NORRIS, Jim	Houston	DT	1962-63
NOVSEK, Joe	Tulsa	DE	1962

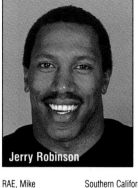

Jerry Robinson

R

RAE, Mike	Southern California	QB	1976-78
RAMSEY, Derrick	Kentucky	TE	1978-83
RATHMAN, Tom	Nebraska	RB	1994
REESE, Archie	Clemson	DT	1982-83
REGENT, Shawn	Boston College	C	1987
REINFELDT, Mike	Wisconsin, Milwaukee	DB	1978
REYNOLDS, Billy	Pittsburgh	QB	1960
REYNOLDS, M.C.	Louisiana State	QB	1961
RICE, Floyd	Alcorn A&M	LB	1976-77
RICE, Harold	Tennessee State	DE	1971
RICE, Ken	Auburn	T	1964-65
RICH, Randy	New Mexico	DB	1978
RIDLEHUBER, Preston	Georgia	RB	1968
RIEHM, Chris	Ohio State	G	1986-88
RIEVES, Charles	Houston	LB	1962-63
RIVERA, Hank	Oregon State	DB	1962
ROBBINS, Austin	North Carolina	DT	1994-95
ROBBINS, Barret	Texas Christian	C	1995-97
ROBERSON, Bo	Cornell	WR	1962-65
ROBERTS, Cliff	Illinois	DT	1961
ROBINSON, Greg	Northeast Louisiana	RB	1993-94
ROBINSON, Jerry	UCLA	LB	1985-91
ROBINSON, Johnny	Louisiana Tech	DT-DE	1981-83
ROBISKIE, Terry	Louisiana State	RB	1977-79
RODERICK, John	Southern Methodist	WR	1968
RODRIGUEZ, Mike	Alabama	DT	1987
ROEDEL, Herb	Marquette	G	1961
ROMANO, Jim	Penn State	C	1982-84
ROSENSTEIL, Bob	Eastern Illinois	TE	1997
ROTHER, Tim	Nebraska	T-DT	1989-90
ROWE, Dave	Penn State	DT	1975-78
RUBKE, Karl	Southern California	DE	1968
RUSSELL, Booker	Southwest Texas State	RB	1978-79
RUSSELL, Darrell	Southern California	DT-DE	1997

Ken Stabler

S

SABAL, Ron	Purdue	T	1960-61
SCHMAUTZ, Ray	San Diego State	LB	1966
SCHROEDER, Jay	UCLA	QB	1988-92
SCHUH, Harry	Memphis State	T	1965-70
SEALE, Sam	Western State (CO.)	WR-DB	1984-87
SEILER, Paul	Notre Dame	T	1971-73

SHAW, Glenn	Kentucky	RB	1963-64
SHEDD, Kenny	Northern Iowa	WR	1996-97
SHELL, Arthur	Maryland State	T	1968-82
SHERMAN, Rod	Southern California	WR	1967, 69-71
SHIPP, Jackie	Oklahoma	LB	1989
SHIRKEY, George	Stephen F. Austin	DT	1962
SIANI, Mike	Villanova	WR	1972-77
SIMPSON, Jack	Mississippi	LB	1962-64
SIMPSON, Willie	San Francisco State	RB	1962
SISTRUNK, Otis	None	DE-DT	1972-79
SKREPENAK, Greg	Michigan	T	1992-95
SLIGH, Richard	North Carolina College	T	1967
SLOUGH, Greg	Southern California	LB	1971-72
SMITH, Anthony	Arizona	DE	1991-97
SMITH, Bubba	Michigan State	DE	1973-74
SMITH, Charles	Utah	RB	1968-74
SMITH, Hal	UCLA	DT	1961
SMITH, James	Compton J.C.	RB	1960
SMITH, Jim	Michigan	WR	1985
SMITH, Jimmy	Elon	RB	1984
SMITH, Kevin	UCLA	TE	1992-94
SMITH, Ron	Wisconsin	DB	1974
SMITH, Steve	Penn State	RB	1987-93
SMITH, Willie	Michigan	RB	1961
SOMMER, Mike	George Washington	RB	1963
SPENCER, Ollie	Kansas	G	1963
SPIVEY, Mike	Colorado	DB	1980
SQUIREK, Jack	Illinois	LB	1982-85
STABLER, Ken	Alabama	QB	1970-79
STALLS, Dave	Northern Colorado	DT	1983, 85
STEINFORT, Fred	Boston College	K	1976
STEPHENS, Rich	Tulsa	G-T	1992-96
STEWART, Joe	Missouri	WR	1978-79
STONE, Jack	Oregon	T	1961-62
STRACHAN, Steve	Boston College	RB	1985-89
STREIGEL, Bill	Pacific	LB	1960
SVIHUS, Bob	Southern California	T	1965-70
SWEENEY, Steve	California	WR	1973
SWILLING, Pat	Georgia Tech	DE	1995-96
SYLVESTER, Steve	Notre Dame	C-G-T	1975-83

Jack Tatum

T

TALLEY, Stan	Texas Christian	K	1987
TATUM, Jack	Ohio State	DB	1971-79
TAUTOLO, John	UCLA	T	1987
TAYLOR, Billy	Texas Tech	RB	1982
TAYLOR, Malcolm	Tennessee State	DT	1987-88
TEAL, Willie	Louisiana State	DB	1987
TERESA, Tony	San Jose State	RB	1960
THOMAS, Skip	Southern California	DB	1972-78
THOMS, Art	Syracuse	DT	1969-76
TILLMON, Tony	Texas	DB	1987
TODD, Larry	Arizona State	RB	1965-70
TOOMAY, Pat	Vanderbilt	DE	1977-79

TORAN, Stacey	Notre Dame	DB	1984-88
TOWNSEND, Greg	Texas Christian	DE-LB	1983-93
TRAPP, James	Clemson	DB	1993-97
TRASK, Orville	Rice	DT	1962
TREU, Adam	Nebraska	G-T	1997
TRUAX, Dalton	Tulane	DT	1960
TRUITT, Olanda	Mississippi State	WR	1996-97
TURK, Dan	Wisconsin	C	1989-96
TURNER, Eric	UCLA	S	1997
TYSON, Richard	Tulsa	G	1966

Gene Upshaw

U

UPSHAW, Gene	Texas A&I	G	1967-82
URENDA, Herman	Pacific	WR	1963

Mark van Eeghen

V

VALDEZ, Vernon	San Diego University	DB	1962
VAN DIVIER, Randy	Washington	G	1982
van EEGHEN, Mark	Colgate	RB	1974-81
VANN, Norwood	East Carolina	LB	1988
VAN PELT, Brad	Michigan State	LB	1984-85
VAUGHAN, Ruben	Colorado	DT-DE	1982
VELLA, John	Southern California	G-T	1972-79
VILLAPIANO, Phil	Bowling Green	LB	1971-79
VOIGHT, Bob	Los Angeles State	DE	1961

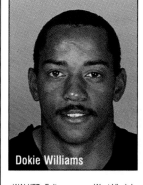

Dokie Williams

W

WALKER, Fulton	West Virginia	DB	1985-86
WALLACE, Aaron	Texas A&M	LB, DE	1990-95, 1997
WARE, Tim	Southern California	WR	1989
WARREN, Jimmy	Illinois	DB	1970-74, 77
WARZEKA, Ron	Montana State	DE	1960
WASHINGTON, Lionel	Tulane	DB	1987-94, 97
WASHINGTON, Ronnie	Northeast Louisiana	LB	1987
WATTS, Robert	Boston College	LB	1978
WATTS, Ted	Texas Tech	DB	1981-84
WAYMER, Dave	Notre Dame	DB	1992
WEATHERS, Carl	San Diego State	LB	1970-71
WEAVER, Gary	Fresno State	LB	1973
WELLS, Warren	Texas Southern	WR	1967-70
WESTBROOKS, Greg	Colorado	LB	1978-81
WHEELER, Dwight	Tennessee State	C-T	1984, 87-88
WHEELER, Ron	Washington	TE	1987
WHITE, Alberto	Texas Southern	DE	1994
WHITE, Eugene	Florida A&M	RB	1982
WHITLEY, Curtis	Clemson	C-G	1997
WHITTAKER, Scott	Kansas	C-T	1997
WHITTINGTON, Arthur	Southern Methodist	RB	1978-81
WILKERSON, Bruce	Tennessee	G-T	1987-94
WILLIAMS, David	Illinois	WR	1987
WILLIAMS, Demise	Oklahoma State	DB	1987
WILLIAMS, Dokie	UCLA	WR	1983-87
WILLIAMS, Harvey	Louisiana State	RB	1994-97
WILLIAMS, Jamie	Nebraska	TE	1994
WILLIAMS, Henry	San Diego State	DB	1979
WILLIAMS, Howie	Howard	DB	1964-69
WILLIAMS, Ricky	Langston	DB	1985
WILLIAMS, Willie	Grambling	DB	1966
WILLIAMSON, Fred	Northwestern	DB	1961-64
WILLIAMSON, J.R	Louisiana Tech	LB	1964-67
WILLIS, Chester	Auburn	RB	1981-84
WILLIS, Mitch	Southern Methodist	DT	1985-87
WILSON, Marc	Brigham Young	QB	1980-87
WILSON, Marcus	Virginia	RB	1991
WILSON, Nemiah	Grambling	DB	1968-74
WILSON, Otis	Louisville	LB	1989
WINANS, Jeff	Southern California	G-DT	1976
WISE, Mike	California-Davis	DE	1986-90
WISNIEWSKI, Steve	Penn State	G	1989-97
WOLFF, Scott	Mt. Union	QB	1987
WOOD, Dick	Auburn	QB	1965
WOODS, Chris	Auburn	WR	1987-88
WRIGHT, Alexander	Auburn	WR	1992-94
WRIGHT, Steve	Northern Iowa	T	1987-93
WYATT, Alvin	Bethune-Cookman	DB	1970
YOUSO, Frank	Minnesota	T	1963-65
ZECHER, Rich	Utah State	T	1965
ZOGG, John	Boise State	G	1987

Canon

NFL Photo of the Year
Super Bowl Sunday 1998
Photography by Rich Clarkson and Associates

$\mathcal{H}$OW MANY FIRST CLASS RESTAURANTS HAVE THIS ON THE MENU?

THE COLISEUM LUXURY SUITES.

A Luxury Suite at the Coliseum will satisfy any appetite for luxury. It's Raider football served up to you on a silver platter. As well as access to the first-class Stadium Clubs, you and your guests can enjoy a feast of football in the comfort of your own exclusive suite.

Relax in comfortable, upholstered, theater-style seats in front of a glass wall which you can retract for an open-air view from the best sightlines in the stadium. Between plays you can take a break and enjoy the suite itself, with its color TVs, refrigerators, kitchen facilities and private restrooms. It's the ultimate gourmet NFL experience. If you're ready for it, call now.

Club Seats and Luxury Suites both offer exclusive advantages including:

Prime midfield plaza-level viewing.

Food and beverage attendant service to your seat.

Seated dining in a first-class restaurant.

Access to two exclusive Stadium Clubs with pre- and post-game hours.

Satellite television sports coverage.

Pregame and halftime shows and autograph signing by Raider Legends.

Preferred parking.

Private, secure stadium entrance and exit.

THE COLISEUM CLUB.

A Coliseum Club Seat lets you see Raider football as you've never seen it before. In the lap of luxury. For starters, you get the best view in the stadium from midfield seats that are so good you won't want to leave them. Luckily, food and drink is brought to you by waiters, so you don't have to. If you do manage to tear yourself away from the action being dished up on the field, you'll find fine food and drink being served at the first class restaurant inside your exclusive Stadium Club. Along with a great sports bar, satellite TV sports coverage and modern, convenient restrooms.

If all that's got you hungry for more, call today. And you could soon be living on a diet of prime Raider football.

CALL 1-888-44RAIDERS
FOR INFORMATION

DOMINATION

The Raiders, at 21-8 in one point games, are pro football's best in the tightest games. But TOTAL DOMINATION by the Raiders in terms of consistent victory for four decades has been accomplished in more than just the close games.

In fact, of the 332 league game wins posted from 1960 through 1997, 70 have been by margins of 20 points of more. That's right, of those 332 Raider wins, 21.1 percent have come by at least three touchdowns. Twenty three of these triumphs have been by 30 points or more and four have even come by more than 40 points.

Sixteen of the Raiders 65 interconference wins against teams from the NFC have come by 20 points or more. And four of the Raiders 33 wins in the Monday Night Football series have been by margins of 20 points or more.

Of the Raiders 332 victories from 1960-1997, 16 have seen the Silver and Black hold their opponents scoreless. Eight of these 16 shutout wins have even come on the road.

And in the very biggest of the big games—the Super Bowls—the Raiders three World Championships of Professional Football have been won by 18 points, 17 points and 29 points.

Consistent victory in every department, though more difficult in recent years, has been a trademark of the Raiders—both in Oakland and while in Los Angeles. In the 13 seasons in Southern California—1982 thru 1994—the Raiders built a 118-82-0 record, including a 64-36-0 mark at home at the mammoth Los Angeles Memorial Coliseum.

Since merged play began in 1970, the record for the Silver and Black in those 28 seasons is 255-163-6.

Over the decades the Raiders have been dominating both at home and on the road. On their own turf, the Raiders 38-year mark from 1960 thru 1997 stood at 184-95-3. On the road, the Raiders 38-year record was 148-126-8, including a winning record in road games played on artificial turf.

The Raiders have a winning record against every one of the six NFL divisions:

64-44-4 versus AFC East
51-32-0 versus AFC Central
151-109-6 versus AFC West
19-12-0 versus NFC East
25-12-0 versus NFC Central
22-12-1 versus NFC West

The Raiders have a winning record in every month of the normal league season, from September thru December:

68-58-1 in September
96-54-6 in October
91-60-3 in November
75- 47-1 in December

And on Monday nights the Raiders remain dominant with a 33-16-1 record.

The Raiders have a winning record for their 38 years of preseason games. The Raiders have a winning record for their 38 years of regular season games. And the Raiders have a winning record for their 18 years of postseason games. The Raiders have a winning record for games played the week after a bye. The Raiders have a winning record for games played after a Monday night game. The Raiders have a winning record in opening day games. The Raiders have a winning record in final games of the season.

The Raiders have a winning record in each of the four decades in which this unique franchise has put a team on the field—the '60s, the '70s, the '80s, and the '90s.

The Raiders are one of only three NFL teams to have played in Championship Games in all four decades from the '60s thru the '90s.

During the 38 memorable years, there have been different players, different coaches, different stadiums, different opponents, but one constant—VICTORY!

JUST WIN, BABY!

In the past fifty years—the modern era of professional football—there have been some great individual seasons that have a special place in the history of the game. Some that stand out are the Miami Dolphins 14-0-0 season in 1972; the Oakland Raiders 13-1-0 record in 1976; the Chicago Bears 15-1-0 mark in 1985; the 11-1-0 season of the Cleveland Browns in '53; the San Francisco 49ers 15-1-0 record in '84; the Los Angeles Raiders and Washington Redskins 8-1-0 records in the strike-shortened 1982 campaign; the Oakland Raiders 12-1-1 record in 1969; the Baltimore Colts 13-1-0 mark in '68 and the Oakland Raiders 13-1-0 record in 1967, for example.

But no team in this fifty-year period ever had three consecutive league seasons as outstanding as the three the Oakland Raiders linked together from 1967 thru 1969:

OAKLAND RAIDERS	
1967	13-1-0
1968	12-2-1
1969	12-1-1
1967-69	37-4-1

That's right! Of 42 league games played by the Raiders in these three memorable seasons, ONLY FOUR WERE LOSSES—37-4-1—the best three-season record for any NFL team since World War II.

This 37-4-1-record required some of the greatest players, the greatest coaches, the greatest plays and the greatest games in the history of professional football. And the 1967, 1968 and 1969 Oakland Raiders met these standards—and then some.

Tackle Harry Schuh and guard Gene Upshaw

Seven members of the Oakland Raider organization during those three great years have been enshrined in the Professional Football Hall of Fame—owner Al Davis, wide receiver Fred Biletnikoff, quarterback-placekicker George Blanda, cornerback Willie Brown, center Jim Otto, offensive tackle Art Shell and guard Gene Upshaw.

Twenty proud wearers of the Silver and Black were chosen to play in the AFL All-Star Game during this 1967-1969 span—safety George Atkinson, wide receiver Fred Biletnikoff, defensive lineman Dan Birdwell, quarterback-placekicker George Blanda, cornerback Willie Brown, tight end Billy Cannon, linebacker Dan Conners, defensive lineman Ben Davidson, running back Hewritt Dixon, safety Dave Grayson, guard Wayne Hawkins, defensive line-

man Tom Keating, quarterback Daryle Lamonica, cornerback Kent McCloughan, linebacker Gus Otto, center Jim Otto, offensive tackle Harry Schuh, guard Gene Upshaw, wide

Defensive lineman Dan Birdwell

Wide receiver Warren Wells

receiver Warren Wells and cornerback Nemiah Wilson.

Two different head coaches led Raider teams in these great seasons. John Rauch coached the 1967 and 1968 Raiders while John Madden

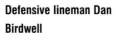

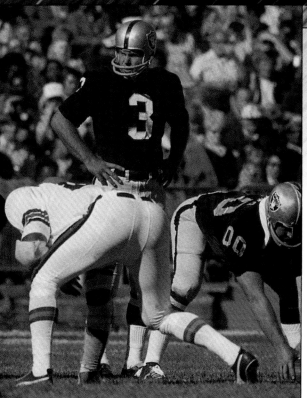

Quarterback Daryle Lamonica and center Jim Otto get ready to attack.

was the coach of the 1969 Raiders. Ron Wolf—now executive vice-president and general manager of the Green Bay Packers—was the director of player personnel who aided managing general partner Al Davis in stocking these teams with dedicated, tough, talent-

ed players.

In 1967 the Oakland Raiders set a club record that still stands, scoring 468 points. In fact, the Raiders led the league in scoring in each of these three seasons. The Raiders set club records with 58 touchdowns in 1967, and with 36 touchdown passes and 5,696 offensive yards in 1969.

As expected, great individual performances occurred during the games played in the 1967-69 period. Quarterback Daryle Lamonica threw for 89 touchdowns in these three seasons, including a Raider record 34 in 1967, and six TDs in a 1969 game against the Buffalo Bills. Wide receiver Warren Wells caught 14 touchdown passes in 1969 and averaged 26.8 yards per catch that season. George Blanda scored over 100 points in each of these seasons, totaling 338 points for the period. And safety Dave Grayson intercepted ten passes in 1968.

Highlighting this three-season span was the

Linebacker Dan Conners

Raiders' American Football League Championship in 1967, when they went on to represent the AFL in Super Bowl II against the NFL Champion Green Bay Packers in the Orange Bowl in Miami, Florida.

The 1967-1968-1969 period—golden years for many, but Silver and Black seasons for professional football.

Safety George Atkinson

1967 [13-1]

9-10	W	51-0	DENVER BRONCOS
9-17	W	35-7	BOSTON PATRIOTS
10- 1	W	23-21	KANSAS CITY CHIEFS
10- 7	L	14-27	at New York Jets
10-15	W	24-20	at Buffalo Bills
10-22	W	48-14	at Boston Patriots
10-29	W	51-10	SAN DIEGO CHARGERS
11- 5	W	21-17	at Denver Broncos
11-19	W	31-17	MIAMI DOLPHINS
11-23	W	44-22	at Kansas City Chiefs
12- 3	W	41-21	at San Diego Chargers
12-10	W	19-7	at Houston Oilers
12-17	W	38-29	NEW YORK JETS
12-24	W	28-21	BUFFALO BILLS

1968 [12-2]

9-15	W	48-6	at Buffalo Bills
9-21	W	47-21	at Miami Dolphins
9-29	W	24-15	at Houston Oilers
10- 6	W	41-10	BOSTON PATRIOTS
10-13	L	14-23	SAN DIEGO CHARGERS
10-20	L	10-24	at Kansas City Chiefs
10-27	W	31-10	CINCINNATI BENGALS
11- 3	W	38-21	KANSAS CITY CHIEFS
1-10	W	43-7	at Denver Broncos
11-17	W	43-32	NEW YORK JETS
11-24	W	34-0	at Cincinnati Bengals
11-28	W	13-10	BUFFALO BILLS
12- 8	W	33-27	DENVER BRONCOS
12-15	W	34-27	at San Diego Chargers

1969 [12-1-1]

9-14	W	21-17	HOUSTON OILERS
9-20	W	20-17	MIAMI DOLPHINS
9-28	W	38-23	at Boston Patriots
10- 4	T	20-20	at Miami Dolphins
10-12	W	24-14	at Denver Broncos
10-19	W	50-21	BUFFALO BILLS
10-26	W	24-12	at San Diego Chargers
11- 2	L	17-31	at Cincinnati Bengals
11- 9	W	41-10	DENVER BRONCOS
11-16	W	21-16	SAN DIEGO CHARGERS
11-23	W	27-24	at Kansas City Chiefs
11-30	W	27-14	at New York Jets
12- 7	W	37-17	CINCINNATI BENGALS
12-13	W	10-6	KANSAS CITY CHIEFS

Tight games, classic comebacks, fantastic finishes, Super Bowl triumphs—all these make for great memories.

But shutouts—when the defense gives your opponent nothing but goose eggs—these too make for memorable moments. Defensive coaches and defensive players especially never forget how beautiful that string of opponent's zeros looks on the scoreboard when the game comes to an end.

Shutouts do not come easily, especially in this era of long-range field-goal kickers. But in their 564 league games from the initial 1960 season through the end of the 1997 campaign, the Raiders have held opponents scoreless 16 times. Eight of these whitewashes have come at home and eight on the road. Fourteen have come against AFC opponents and two against NFC teams. One took place in a Monday Night Football game when the Silver and Black shutout the Oilers, 34-0, in Houston on October 9, 1972. In two different years—1975 and 1992—the Raiders recorded two shutout wins in a single season.

The Raiders biggest margin of victory in a shutout was 51 points in the opening game of the 1967 season when they crushed the visiting Denver Broncos, 51-0, to ignite a season that finished in the Super Bowl. The tightest shutout win for the Raiders was a 6-0 squeaker in San Diego against the Chargers on October 5, 1975. These San Diego Chargers are the most frequent victims for Raider shutouts, having been kept off the scoreboard completely five times.

RAIDER SHUTOUT VICTORIES (1960-1997)

Date	Score	Opponent & Site
12-16-62	20-0	BOSTON PATRIOTS
9-10-67	51-0	DENVER BRONCOS
11-24-68	34-0	at Cincinnati Bengals
9-26-71	34-0	at San Diego Chargers
10-9-72	34-0	at Houston Oilers
11-4-73	42-0	NEW YORK GIANTS
9-29-74	17-0	at Pittsburgh Steelers
10-5-75	6-0	at San Diego Chargers
10-26-75	25-0	SAN DIEGO CHARGERS
12-12-76	24-0	at San Diego Chargers
9-18-77	24-0	SAN DIEGO CHARGERS
9-8-85	31-0	NEW YORK JETS
9-13-87	20-0	at Green Bay Packers
9-15-91	16-0	INDIANAPOLIS COLTS
10-18-92	19-0	at Seattle Seahawks
11-22-92	24-0	DENVER BRONCOS

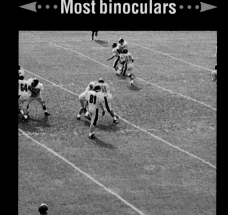

PUT A WILD SPIN ON YOUR ORLANDO VACATION!

TWISTER
RIDE IT OUT℠

Step into one of the most action-packed movies of all time: TWISTER! Grab onto the railing and "Ride It Out," as the swirling vortex of a tornado blows you away!

TO BOOK UNIVERSAL STUDIOS® VACATION PACKAGES, CALL 770-952-8181 ext. 111

UNIVERSAL STUDIOS FLORIDA®

Every game is a challenge to NFL coaching staffs. Preparation is time consuming. Preparation is tedious. Preparation is intense.

But preparing is not enough. You must prepare to win, not just prepare to play!

Success in tight games is one way to measure the success of pro football organizations, their coaching staffs and player personnel. And no measurement of winning the tight ones is more significant than how a team does in games decided by the very slimmest of margins—one point. In these one-point games—games in which every play and every player, every move and countermove—can be decisive—no National Football League team has even come close to the unbelieveable success rate achieved by the Oakland Raiders.

In the 38-year span from 1960 through 1997, the Raiders have been in 29 games decided by just a single point. And in these nail biters, the Raiders success rate is .724, with 21 wins and only eight losses. No other NFL team for this 1960-1997 period came within 35 percentage points of the Silver and Black. ◆

WIN-LOSS RECORDS IN ONE-POINT GAMES (1960-1997)

Rank	Team	Wins	Losses	Percentage
1.	OAKLAND RAIDERS	21	8	.724
2.	Seattle Seahawks	11	5	.688
3.	Indianapolis Colts	18	9	.667
3.	Jacksonville Jaguars	2	1	.667
5.	Dallas Cowboys	12	8	.600
6.	Chicago Bears	20	14	.588
7.	Miami Dolphins	11	8	.579
8.	San Diego Chargers	12	10	.545
9.	New York Jets	14	11	.542
10.	Green Bay Packers	14	12	.538
11.	Minnesota Vikings	17	15	.531
12.	Baltimore Ravens	1	1	.500
12.	Buffalo Bills	9	9	.500
12.	Denver Broncos	10	10	.500
15.	Arizona Cardinals	10	11	.476
15.	Detroit Lions	10	11	.476
17.	Cleveland Browns	9	10	.474
17.	New England Patriots	9	10	.474
17.	Tampa Bay Buccaneers	9	10	.474
20.	Philadelphia Eagles	16	18	.471
21.	Pittsburgh Steelers	7	8	.467
22.	St. Louis Rams	6	7	.462
23.	New Orleans Saints	11	13	.458
24.	New York Giants	8	10	.444
25.	San Francisco 49ers	11	14	.440
26.	Washington Redskins	9	13	.409
27.	Atlanta Falcons	9	14	.391
28.	Cincinnati Bengals	5	9	.357
29.	Tennessee Oilers	7	13	.350
30.	Kansas City Chiefs	9	26	.257
31.	Carolina Panthers	0	0	.000

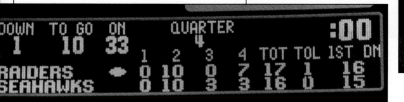

Tim Brown with one of his 10 pass receptions

the road. The temperature hovered near the freezing mark. The field surface was artificial. Sold-out Rich Stadium was a sea of Buffalo Blue and Red as 80,000 upstate New Yorkers badly wanted to destroy their California visitors.

Raider head coach Art Shell—himself a participant in so many big games in 15 seasons as a Pro Football Hall of Fame offensive tackle for the Raiders— had his squad primed and ready.

"We know we've got to win in December if we're going to be in the playoffs, so this is just like a playoff game," said Raider safety Eddie Anderson before the contest began. "We've got to play every game left like it's the playoffs." Buffalo had "blue chip" personnel. Eleven of their 1992 squad had gone to the Pro Bowl.

They were strong on offense, defense and special teams, with no weaknesses. And at home they were near invincible.

Three first-year Raiders were starters on offense and one on defense—veterans Jeff Hostetler at quarterback, Gerald Perry at offensive left tackle and middle linebacker Joe Kelly plus rookie halfback Greg Robinson.

Starting the game on defense, the Raiders pressured early, forcing Buffalo to punt the ball after the minimum three plays. The Silver and Black then drove downfield, primarily on the ground, with Robinson the principal ball carrier. Buffalo's defense stiffened and a Jeff Jaeger field goal from 37 yards out put the Raiders on the scoreboard first, 3-0, midway thru quarter one.

Buffalo blocked the next Jeff Jaeger field goal try early in the second quarter, then marched 80 yards to go ahead 7-3. The touchdown came on a three-yard burst inside by Thurman Thomas.

Later in the second quarter, the Raiders went 72 yards in seven plays to retake the lead, 10-7. Three of the plays were pass completions from Jeff Hostetler to wide receiver Tim Brown for 11, 19 and 37 yards. The final 11 yards and the touchdown came on a scramble to the right side by the mobile Hostetler.

The Raider lead was short-lived, however. Buffalo QB Jim Kelly quickly took his Bills 81 yards in just four plays, with the score coming on a 65-yard pass to wide receiver Don Beebe down the right sideline. Buffalo took a 14-10 lead to the locker room at halftime.

The Raider offense roared out of the dressing room in high gear. In 12 plays they covered 64

Big games were nothing new to the Raiders. Not after four Super Bowls. Not after 34 playoff games. Not after 300 league victories.

But this December trip to cold, gray Buffalo was certainly a big game. The 1993 season was in the balance for the Raiders who were 6-5-0 with five games left to play. The Raiders could now afford few, if any, losses if their Silver and Black banner were to fly during the playoffs for the 18th year in Raider history. Buffalo was a tough, talented, proven opponent. They were 8-3-0 in '93, and the defending AFC Champions for the past three years. They were 45-11-0 since the start of the 1990 league season. But one of those rare losses had come at the hands of the Raiders the year before, 20-3, in the Los Angeles Memorial Coliseum.

The challenges for the Raiders were many. This was their third consecutive game on

RAIDER STARTING LINEUPS

Offense				Defense		
WR	89	ALEXANDER WRIGHT		LE	75	HOWIE LONG
LT	71	GERALD PERRY		LT	91	CHESTER MCGLOCKTON
LG	76	STEVE WISNIEWSKI		RT	74	NOLAN HARRISON
C	72	DON MOSEBAR		RE	93	GREG TOWNSEND
RG	65	MAX MONTOYA		LLB	51	AARON WALLACE
RT	68	BRUCE WILKERSON		MLB	57	JOE KELLY
TE	88	ETHAN HORTON		RLB	99	WINSTON MOSS
WR	81	TIM BROWN		LCB	36	TERRY MCDANIEL
QB	15	JEFF HOSTETLER		RCB	48	LIONEL WASHINGTON
RB	35	STEVE SMITH		SS	20	DERRICK HOSKINS
RB	28	GREG ROBINSON		FS	33	EDDIE ANDERSON

yards and narrowed the Buffalo lead to only one, 14-13, when Jeff Jaeger drilled a 34-yard field goal.

The Bills responded immediately, moving downfield in big yardage chunks. But an intense pass rush and tight coverage by cornerback Terry McDaniel forced Buffalo to go the field-goal route to regain a four-point lead, 17-13, with 4:28 left to play in the third quarter.

Jeff Hostetler rallied the Raiders, scrambling twice for 12 and 10 yards. Again, however, the Bills stopped the visiting Raiders in close and forced them to settle for a 26-yard field goal, to pull within one point again, 17-16, as the third quarter came to an end.

A pass interference call provided big yardage on Buffalo's next possession, and the Bills capitalized as Thurman Thomas swept left for one yard and the touchdown to put Buffalo ahead by eight, 24-16.

The Raiders failed to move the ball, and the Bills took over on their own 40, looking to move in and score three or seven and to take valuable

time off the game clock. But determined Raider defenders had other plans. The upfront crew of Howie Long, Chester McGlockton, Nolan Harrison and Greg Townsend pressured. Corner Terry McDaniel intercepted a Jim Kelly pass intended for Bill Brooks and brought it back 36 yards. Tough defense by the Bills again left head coach Art Shell no choice but to go for the field goal. Jaeger was good again—this time from 47 yards—to cut the Buffalo lead to just five points, 24-19, with 8:47 remaining in the battle. The Raiders running attack had been slowed appreciably, however, by the loss earlier in the game of outstanding rookie back Greg Robinson with a serious knee injury. Running back Napoleon McCallum was also not available, recovering from an emergency apendectomy just a week earlier.

The Bills, with 80,000 bundled-up fans cheering them on, began to drive downfield, knowing that even a field goal would put them up by eight and provide an almost-insurmountable obstacle for the Raiders.

The Raider defense met the challenge, stopped the Bills and silenced the huge crowd. Tight coverage by veteran corner Lionel Washington helped force a punt situation and gave the Raiders the ball back.

Throughout the game, wide receiver Tim Brown had been returning to the huddle telling Jeff, Hostetler, "I can get open."

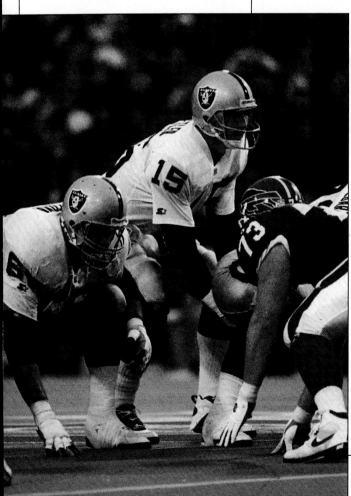

Quarterback Jeff Hostetler led the Raiders to almost 400 yards on offense against Buffalo.

Hostetler couldn't agee more.

"The more time Timmy and I spend together, the better we'll become. You start knowing what a guy's thinking about before he comes out of his cut."

A 15-yard punt return by Brown had put the Raiders 57 yards from the end zone. Completions to Nick Bell for 18 yards and James Jett for ten more cut that down to 29 yards. Then a Hostetler pass to Brown at the goal line on the right side got the 29 yards and a 25-24 lead, after the extra-point attempt was blocked.

Back came the resilient Bills, moving into range for the field goal to go ahead. But before that field position could be earned, defensive tackle Nolan Harrison forced a fumble by Thurman Thomas that safety Eddie Anderson covered on the Raiders 36-yard line.

"I grabbed him with one arm and went for the ball with the other, like we've been working on all year," said Harrison. "I brought the hammer down!"

"The turnovers happened at a time when we needed something to get us going," pointed out Terry McDaniel.

But 2:49 was left to play—an eternity by NFL standards. The Raiders needed to move the ball—and the clock. And that's exactly what the Raiders did. Runs by Nick Bell and then a clutch third-and-five pass for eight yards from Hostetler to Brown kept the ball in Raider hands. Tim Brown had now caught ten passes for a career-best of 183 yards. The Raiders had gained nearly 400 yards and made 25 first downs enroute to this hard-fought 25-24 triumph on the road. And the road to the playoffs got a lot wider. Another classic Raider comeback had paved the way.

"This is probably the worst loss of the season as far as I'm concerned," said Buffalo All Pro defensive lineman Bruce Smith after the game. "It just doesn't add up."

It adds up alright, once you realize that at this point in 1993 the Raiders record in one-point games is 20 wins against only four losses. And that's a .833 winning percentage for the guys in the Silver and Black!

During the 1967-1969 period the Oakland Raiders grew into the most dominant team in professional football in terms of consistent victory, with an incredible three-year record of 37-4-1. Only four losses in 42 league games for Al Davis' organization.

A huge national audience became accustomed to following the Raiders on NBC Television every Sunday. No team in professional football provided the big plays, big hits, wide open offense, attacking defense, great players and great coaches that became a Sunday staple for television fans of the famed, feared Silver and Black.

Yet one of the most legendary games of the nearly 600 league and postseason games played by the Raiders became a landmark in pro football history because people could not see the classic comeback viewed only by the 53,118 fans in the Oakland Coliseum. The wild finish to this New York Jets—Oakland Raiders game on November 17, 1968, was lost to millions of fans when NBC chose instead to show

Big Ben Davidson pressures Jets QB Joe Namath.

the children's classic, "Heidi," as scheduled at 7 p.m., EST. Only those in attendance in Oakland got to share the finish of one of the most exciting contests in pro football history in this next-to-the-last season of the AFL.

The game started slowly with field goals the center of attraction. George Blanda was wide right on a 50-yard attempt on Oakland's first series. A sack of

Jets quarterback Joe Namath by Dan Birdwell slowed one New York drive. Jim Turner then kicked a 44-yard field goal. The Jets recovered a fumble on the Raiders first offensive play in the next series. But on third down New York tight end Pete Lammons was tackled short of the first down, by linebacker Gus Otto, and New York was forced to again settle for a field goal and a 6-0 lead.

The Raiders then put together an 80-yard course to pay dirt. Quarterback Daryle Lamonica opened with a 22-yard pass to wide receiver Warren Wells. Fullback Hewritt Dixon then blasted off tackle for 13 yards behind blocks by guard Jim Harvey, tackle Harry Schuh and tight end Billy Cannon. Lamonica next went to wide receiver Fred Biletnikoff for 15. Dixon

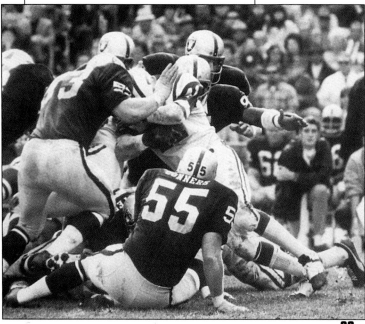

Raider defenders shut down the Jets ground game.

got nine on a draw play. The Raiders moved goalward with precision and purpose. The drive concluded with a nine-yard scoring pass from Lamonica to Wells. The first quarter closed with the Raiders up, 7-6.

narrowed the margin to 14-12 as Namath closed out a 73-yard drive by sneaking in from the Raider one. With the two-point option then available in the AFL, Jets coach Weeb Eubank chose to fake the kick. Holder Babe Parilli tried to pass for the two points and a tie, but an alert Raider defense prevented the completion.

A Jets interception cut short the Raiders initial second half possession and set New York up on the Oakland 30. In four plays, Namath led his team to the end zone, with Bill Mathis powering over from the one to move the Jets ahead, 19-14.

Later in the third quarter the Raiders marched 80 yards to retake the lead. The nine-play drive ended with rookie halfback Charlie Smith, a speedster with size from the University of Utah, going over left

tackle from the three for the touchdown. On the extra point George Blanda faked the kick and holder Daryle Lamonica passed to Hewritt Dixon for two points. Raider head coach John Rauch had completely surprised the Jets to put the Silver and Black ahead, 22-19.

A 50-yard punt return by safety Rodger Bird gave Oakland good field position as the third quarter ended. But a fumble at the Jets three abruptly halted the drive. Namath cashed in on his good fortune and threw to wide receiver Don Maynard for 47 yards on the first play, then came right back to Maynard for 50 yards and a touchdown on the very next play. Turner's extra point and the Jets regained the lead, 26-22, just 45 seconds into the fourth quarter.

In their next possession, the Jets began with 80 yards to go—and got 75. Raider defensive back Warren Powers broke up a third down pass from the Oakland five, forcing New York to take the field-goal route to take a 29-22 lead with 8:49 remaining.

The tenacious Raiders surged back, traveling 88 yards in just eight plays to tie the score at 29 all with only 3:15 left to play. The drive opened brilliantly on a 65-yard touchdown pass over the middle from Lamonica to Smith coming out of the backfield. But a yellow flag brought this one back—nullified by a holding penalty. Lamonica then fully utilized the Raiders varied passing attack, getting completions to Biletnikoff, Smith and Cannon before covering

Halfback Charlie Smith enroute to the go-ahead touchdown in the fourth quarter.

The Raiders moved quickly to widen their lead as the second quarter opened. A beautifully executed screen pass to Billy Cannon—converted from a Heisman Trophy winning running back to a Pro Bowl tight end by Al Davis—covered the final 48 yards. The PAT put the Raiders ahead 14-6.

Late in the quarter the Jets

RAIDER STARTING LINEUPS

Offense			Defense		
WR	81	WARREN WELLS	LE	77	IKE LASSITER
LT	76	BOB SVIHUS	LT	53	DAN BIRDWELL
LG	63	GENE UPSHAW	RT	75	CARLETON OATS
C	00	JIM OTTO	RE	83	BEN DAVIDSON
RG	70	JIM HARVEY	LLB	56	RALPH OLIVER
RT	79	HARRY SCHUH	MLB	55	DAN CONNERS
TE	33	BILLY CANNON	RLB	34	GUS OTTO
WR	25	FRED BILETNIKOFF	LCB	43	GEORGE ATKINSON
QB	3	DARYLE LAMONICA	RCB	24	WILLIE BROWN
RB	40	PETE BANASZAK	SS	21	RODGER BIRD
RB	35	HEWRITT DIXON	FS	45	DAVE GRAYSON

the final 22 yards on a touchdown toss to Biletnikoff, to again tie the score.

With the ball in the hands of "Broadway Joe"—a future Pro Football Hall of Fame enshrinee—the Jets immediately went to work to break the tie. A 42-yard completion to Maynard, combined with a roughing the passer penalty against the Raiders, put the New Yorkers on the Oakland 18. But the Raider defense rose to the challenge and Jim Tumer had to kick a 26-yard field goal to put his Jets ahead again, 32-29, with only 65 seconds left to play.

This great game, well worth remembering for its exciting football display, now moved into the "legend" class. For after the Jets field goal, NBC ran a commercial and the clock in their New York City television headquarters came up on 7 p.m. According to the story circulated later, the descision-maker on duty there was unable to reach any top executive and decided to go with "Heidi," as scheduled, and not carry the game to its completion. So instead of "Broadway Joe," "Mad Bomber" Lamonica and the mean, nasty guys in Silver and Black, America got blonde hair, Swiss Alps and a herd of goats.

What the heck, there were only 65 seconds to go with the Jets ahead 32-29. What could happen, anyway? But anyone back in New York City who thought that way just didn't understand the traditions of the Oakland Raiders. For under those battle-scarred helmets with the sinister pirate logo, were tough, dedicated athletes who in just nine years had built an already unrivaled record of comebacks. Adversity fueled a fire storm of need to win in the hearts and minds of these proud Raiders. In half a decade, Al Davis had taken a franchise on the edge of disaster and turned it into one that was respected, imitated—and feared.

While NBC viewers got yodels from "Heidi," the sellout crowd at the Oakland Coliseum were on their feet cheering. Lamonica threw to Charlie Smith for 20 yards. A face mask penalty on New York added 15 more. Then Lamonica again passed to Smith streaking to the right. Smith put it in high gear, pulling away from New York pursuers as he sped along the right

Charlie Smith heads back from the end zone after putting the Raiders ahead for good.

sideline, going 43 yards for the go-ahead touchdown. Blanda's point-after put the Raiders ahead 36-32 with 42 seconds left in the game.

On both sidelines coaches huddled with their squads to plot strategy for the Jets offense and Raiders defense. But the New York offense never got the chance to fight back. On the kickoff by Mike Eischied, Jets safety Earl Christy fielded the ball on the ten, then fumbled and couldn't pick up the ball cleanly as swarming Raider special teamers closed in. Reserve running back Preston Ridlehuber grabbed the skidding football on the Jets two and stumbled into the end zone for an Oakland touchdown. The Coliseum became an absolute madhouse. Fans hollered and jumped and embraced. Their Raiders had done it again. Blanda kicked the point and the Oakland Raiders put this wonderful afternoon of football into their win column, 43-32.

NBC Television had been receiving calls of complaint since they had deserted Oakland for Switzerland with 1:05 left to play. But a few minutes later when a graphic ran across the bottom of television screens everywhere, superimposing the final score over the Heidi scene, their switchboard lit up like a Christmas tree. FINAL SCORE: OAKLAND RAIDERS 43—NEW YORK JETS 32, it read. And the "Heidi Game" was added to Raider history and sports vocabulary.

Julian Goodman, NBC President, later commented: "It was a forgivable error committed by human beings who were concerned about the children expecting to see "Heidi" at 7 p.m. I missed the end of the game as much as anyone."

Soon thereafter, however, NBC issued a statement to the fans—and an order to their staff and personnel. From this time on, NFL games would "be shown in their entirety."

Once again the Raiders had altered the course of football history.

OfficeMax®

reat players, great coaches, great plays, great games and great leadership have been constant threads in the weaving of the Raiders unmatched fabric of excellence. Uncommon valor has been a common virtue among the countless heroes who have proudly worn the Silver and Black over these memorable four decades. Second effort has been first nature for the exceptional men who have built and nurtured the Raider tradition of greatness.

Extraordinary tight games and unforgettable finishes have become a Raider way of life in these historic decades. No National Football League team comes close to the Raiders record of success in these most thrilling games. The Raiders record of 21 wins against only eight losses in one-point decisions from 1960 through 1997 is labeled by many as "miraculous." But there are few true miracles in the NFL. This record is the result of meticulous planning and preparation, of class and courage, of mind and muscle, daring and decisiveness by dedicated people—people with an unyielding commitment to excellence.

Classic comebacks have become a well-established Raider tradition. Over the four decades since the Raider franchise came into existence as an afterthought—a last minute replacement for another area that dropped out after being enticed by the older National Football League—the Raiders have thundered down the stretch. They have conquered challenges and challengers in fourth quarters, home or away, outdoors or inside, on grass or artificial turf, in the mud or dust or on frozen fields, against all odds.

Widely-scattered alien sites such as Mile High Stadium in Denver, RFK Stadium in our nation's capital, San Diego Jack Murphy Stadium, Candlestick Park in San Francisco, the Kingdome in Seattle, Giants Stadium in East Rutherford, New Jersey, Anaheim Stadium, the Humphrey Metrodome in Minnesota, ancient Soldier Field in Chicago, Pontiac Silverdome outside Detroit, Arrowhead Stadium in Kansas City—these and many others have seen battle-hardened fighters in Silver and Black buckle on their helmets and storm goalward to add victory to history.

In the first 78 years of play in the National Football League teams have overcome deficits of 24 points or more only a dozen times or so in the roughly 10,000 games played. Two of those dozen greatest comebacks were wins by the Raiders. But whether its come-from-behind or stay-out-in front, whether it's home or away, in the renovated Oakland Coliseum or on foreign soil, whatever the odds, whoever the foe—RAIDER WILL TO WIN WILL ENDURE FOREVER.

Tradition, continuity, a sense of history—these are meaningful things to owner Al Davis and the Raider organization. Building their great record, first in Oakland, then in Los Angeles, and finally back in Oakland, the Raiders have utilized the rock-solid foundation of past glories as a roadway for the future.

Pro football fans in the sprawling Los Angeles area had become aware of the Raiders come-from-behind tradition primarily through televised games featuring the Silver and Black as they dominated pro football in Oakland. But then, in 1982—the Raiders first season in Los Angeles—these Southern California football fans finally would live through Raider classic comebacks up close and personal.

The Raiders had opened the '82 league season on the road, first downing the San Francisco 49ers in Candlestick Park on Sunday, September 12, by a 23-17 score. The next Sunday the Raiders had traveled to Atlanta's Fulton County Stadium to crush the Falcons, 38-14.

Then came a bitter 57-day NFL players strike that stretched until late November. The NFL had been forced to cancel weekends of league play. Scrubbed for the Raiders had been four home games and four more on the road.

Finally, on Monday night, November 22, 1982, the Raiders would make their league debut at home in the Los Angeles Memorial Coliseum. The opponent would be a long-time division rival—the San Diego Chargers. For this 45th meeting between the Raiders and Chargers, the Raiders were 2-0-0 in '82 and the Chargers 1-1-0.

Among the vast array of statistics circulated before this historic Raider debut in Los Angeles, one stood out. The Raiders

Linebackers Rod Martin and Ted Hendricks lead swarming Raider defense.

were the undisputed "Kings of Monday Night Football," with an incredible record of 18 wins and one tie against only two losses in the 21 games they had played in this prime-time national television series that had changed the viewing habits of an entire nation since its inception in 1970. But one of those two Monday night losses had come the year before at the hands of the Chargers, 23-10, in San Diego.

The wide-open Charger offense, tutored by head coach Don Coryell and quarterbacked by talented Dan Fouts, got on the board first—and often—in the opening half.

San Diego went in front 3-0 on a field goal

by one-time Raider draft choice Rolf Benirschke. Later in the first period, the Chargers stretched their lead to 10-0 on a 29-yard scoring pass from Fouts to wide receiver Dwight Scales.

The Chargers scored twice more in the second stanza on short runs by Chuck Muncie. The crowd grew restless—and with considerable reason. For the Raiders now trailed 24-0 and had never previously overcome a 24-point deficit. But just before the half, the Raiders' offense came to life, as did the Coliseum crowd.

After a missed field goal by Chris Bahr, the Raider defense quickly got the ball back for the offense when future Pro Football Hall of Fame linebacker Ted Hendricks recovered a Charger fumble on the San Diego 17-yard line with only 1:19 left to play in the first half. Quarterback Jim Plunkett passed to rookie running back Marcus Allen for 11 yards. Allen fumbled the pitchout on the very next play but fortunately made the recovery, losing six yards. Plunkett passed to Allen again for 11 yards. Finally, with 42 seconds left, Plunkett scrambled free from a San Diego rush and popped a short pass to tight end Todd Christensen from one yard out, to bring the Raiders within 17 points at halftime. Chargers 24-Raiders 7.

RAIDER STARTING LINEUPS

Offense			Defense		
WR	21	CLIFF BRANCH	LE	73	DAVE BROWNING
LT	79	BRUCE DAVIS	NT	62	REGGIE KINLAW
LG	60	CURT MARSH	RE	77	LYLE ALZADO
C	50	DAVE DALBY	LLB	83	TED HENDRICKS
RG	65	MICKEY MARVIN	MLB	55	MATT MILLEN
RT	70	HENRY LAWRENCE	RLB	53	ROD MARTIN
TE	46	TODD CHRISTENSEN	LCB	37	LESTER HAYES
WR	80	MALCOLM BARNWELL	RCB	20	TED WATTS
QB	16	JIM PLUNKETT	XCB	23	ODIS McKINNEY
RB	32	MARCUS ALLEN	SS	36	MIKE DAVIS
RB	33	KENNY KING	FS	44	BURGESS OWENS

Linebacker Matt Millen gets upfield with a Charger turnover.

Head coach Tom Flores—himself a veteran of Raider comebacks as a player, assistant coach and head coach—rallied his squad at halftime.

"Among other things, I reminded them that this was Monday Night Football with the eyes of an entire nation on us," recalls Coach Flores. "Monday Night magic—I don't know what it is about it. We're very proud of our Monday Night record. Monday Night Football brings out the best in us."

Early in the third quarter, a sack of Fouts by Ted Hendricks shut down a San Diego series. After the punt, the Raiders took over on their own 36. Jim Plunkett found Christensen open over the middle on consecutive gains of 11 and 12 yards. Kenny King then carried four times for 24 yards, setting up a Marcus Allen three-yard burst inside for the touchdown to cut the San Diego lead to 10 points, 24-14.

Dan Fouts came back, firing but Odis McKinney, playing as the fifth defensive back in the Raiders "Pirate" coverage, forced a fumble by San Diego tight end Kellen Winslow on a screen pass, with defensive lineman Ruben Vaughan gaining possession for the Silver and Black. King and Allen shared the rushing duties as the huge Raider front line of center Dave Dalby, guards Mickey Marvin and Curt Marsh and tackles Henry Lawrence and Bruce Davis began to dominate the line of scrimmage. A middle

trap sprung King for 21 yards, and then Allen swept right for six yards and the touchdown at 2:23 left in the third quarter. The Chargers now led by only three, 24-21.

Booming punts by the incomparable Ray Guy kept San Diego at bay, as did the play of the alert secondary of corners Lester Hayes and Ted Watts, safeties Mike Davis and Burgess Owens and extra DB's Odis McKinney, James Davis and Vann McElroy. A sack by Ruben Vaughan snuffed out a San Diego threat. Then a missed field goal gave the Raiders the ball on their own 20 with 9:55 left to play.

Plunkett marched his forces goalward, beginning with a 14-yard completion to Cliff Branch, followed by receptions by Todd Christensen for 24 and 13 yards. An end-around by super-swift wide receiver Malcolm Barnwell netted 14 yards. Two plays later fullback Frank Hawkins slanted over from the one to put the Raiders ahead—finally—28-24. But there was still nearly six minutes remaining.

An interception by rookie safety Vann McElroy with 1:56 showing on the clock shut San Diego down again. A series of runs by King and Allen took time off the clock. San Diego got one final play, but corner Lester Hayes batted down Fouts' last effort to get the ball to Charlie Joiner in the end zone. The frenzied Coliseum crowd roared approval as their Raiders had come from 24 points down to score a 28-24 victory in their very first home league game.

In the noisy, crowded dressing room after the game guard Mickey Marvin, a veteran of the Super Bowl XV win two years earlier said, "We've gained some fans who have now learned not to leave before the end. With us it

often goes down to the wire. The Raiders have been doing this for a long time, since before I came in 1977."

Kenny King summed the win up by saying, "I definitely think we won ourselves some fans in our new home. I saw some of the other NFL games that were on TV yesterday, and I don't think they compared at all to the game we gave the fans out there tonight. I think this was one of the better

Linebacker Ted Hendricks puts the squeeze on Charger quarterback Dan Fouts.

Monday night games they've ever had on."

One of the better games, perhaps, but just one more in the Raider tradition of classic comebacks. Home or away, Sunday, Monday, Thursday or Saturday, day or night, outdoors or indoors—classic comebacks like this are part and parcel of the undeniable greatness of the Raiders.

In the first 69 years of play in the National Football League, one of the true rarities was a comeback victory by a team 24 points behind in the game. In the thousands of league games played between the NFL's start in 1920 and September 26, 1988, a 24-point comeback had been topped only twice. And it had happened only once in a Monday Night Football game!

But rallying from 24 points behind—and with only one half of the game remaining—was the task facing the injury-riddled Los Angeles Raiders in hostile, sold-out Mile High Stadium in Denver on that September evening.

Yet, the setting was right for the Raiders. This was Monday Night Football, a domain ruled by the Silver and Black. Ever since this ABC prime-time national television series began in 1970, the Raiders had built an incredible record of 25-5-1 in the 19 years of these Monday evening specials. In fact, at one point the Raiders had won 14 Monday night contests in a row over a period of 11 years.

In 1988, however, 16 Raider players were already on injured reserve only three games into the season. Proven starters like cornerback Terry McDaniel, safety Vann McElroy and guard Brian Holloway were gone. Safety Stacey Toran, cornerback Lionel Washington and center Don Mosebar remained on the active roster but were unable to play in Denver because of injuries. The Silver and Black had come up black and blue.

Quarterback Jay Schroeder—newly arrived, recently acquired in a trade from the defending Super Bowl Champion Washington Redskins—would get his first start since joining the Raiders. Rory Graves would be in only his second pro start at the key offensive left tackle spot. Likewise for rookie Dennis Price at left corner.

For first-year Raider head coach Mike Shanahan this was a very special night. After four years as offensive coordinator for the Denver Broncos, Shanahan was returning to Mile High Stadium as field boss of the Broncos arch-rival for 29 seasons—the hated Raiders.

A tight game was predicted. After all, though the Raiders had totally dominated the league series against Denver, with a 36-17-2 record, the Broncos had won the last four games. Three of the last seven matches between these AFC Western Division rivals, both original American Football League entries, had gone into overtime.

The visiting Raiders got field position early when 13-year veteran corner Mike Haynes—a future Pro Football Hall of Fame member—intercepted a John Elway pass and returned it to the Denver 31. Jay Schroeder's first play as a Raider was a complete suprise to the 76,180 in attendance and to the millions in the huge national television audience—a quarterback draw for 11 yards. First down on the Denver 20.

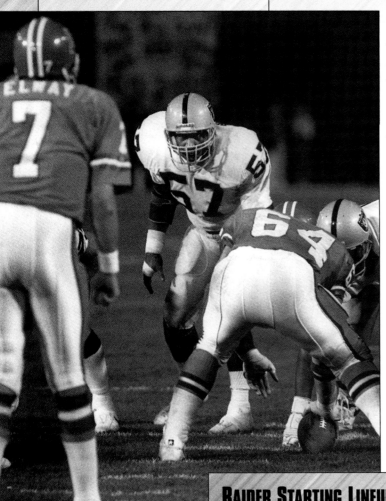

Linebacker Jerry Robinson readies to rush Denver's John Elway.

Raider Starting Lineups

Offense			Defense		
WR	83	WILLIE GAULT	LE	75	HOWIE LONG
LT	60	RORY GRAVES	NT	71	BILL PICKEL
LG	73	CHARLIE HANNAH	RE	90	MIKE WISE
C	51	BILL LEWIS	LLB	54	REGGIE McKENZIE
RG	68	BRUCE WILKERSON	ILB	55	MATT MILLEN
RT	66	STEVE WRIGHT	ILB	57	JERRY ROBINSON
TE	46	TODD CHRISTENSEN	RLB	53	ROD MARTIN
WR	80	JAMES LOFTON	LCB	38	DENNIS PRICE
QB	13	JAY SCHROEDER	RCB	22	MIKE HAYNES
RB	35	STEVE SMITH	SS	30	STACEY TORAN
RB	32	MARCUS ALLEN	FS	33	EDDIE ANDERSON

Tight end Todd Christiansen gets open short against the Broncos.

Three plays later this first Raider trip downfield ended abruptly when Denver linebacker Simon Fletcher picked off a Schroeder pass out of shotgun formation.

Four plays later the Broncos brought their fans to their feet and took a 7-0 lead. An 86-yard pass play from Elway to wide receiver Vance Johnson and a one-yard burst by Tony Dorsett lit the scoreboard. And that's how the first quarter ended.

One play into the second period, Dorsett scored again. Denver up 14-0. Nine minutes later it was Broncos 21-Raiders 0. And a 39-yard field goal by Rich Karlis made it 24-0, Denver ahead convincingly, at halftime.

As the ABC-TV trio of Al Michaels, Frank Gifford and Dan Dierdorf took their caustic shots at the Raiders, almost laughing at the team's first half ineptness, the players and coaches gath-

ered in the dressing room deep under the grandstand.

Six seasons earlier, in 1982, at the Los Angeles Memorial Coliseum, the Raiders had overcome a 24-0 deficit to defeat the San Diego Chargers, 28-24, in another Monday night game. But like tight end Todd Christensen said later, "That was San Diego." Correct, Todd. This was Denver, and Mile High Stadium where the Broncos had not been beaten in 27 consecutive games when leading at the end of the third quarter.

"We stunk it up in the first half," commented veteran linebacker Rod Martin. "It was horrible. Pitiful."

Coach Shanahan told his troops that every player and coach in that Raider dressing room had to be embarrassed by their play in the first half. Defensive coach Charlie Sumner, a veteran of three decades with the organization, told his group that it was the worst half of football he had ever seen the Raiders play.

The statistics certainly bore out those statements. Denver had 16 first downs and 289 yards on offense to three first downs and a paltry 41 yards for the Raiders. The Raiders had punted five times already, the Broncos not even once. Tony Dorsett had rushed for 66 yards and Sammy Winder for 68. The Raiders rushers totaled 22 yards. Schroeder had completed just two of his eight passes, Elway eight of 11. Denver's Vance Johnson had already gained 110 yards receiving while the Raiders totaled a scant 26 yards thru the air.

The first 30 minutes of gloom and doom were done, but 30 more minutes—at least—remained to play.

Cornerback Mike Haynes returns a pass interception.

$3.00 Music & Video Cash checks, inside specially-marked Sony products!

- Checks are good for $3.00 off the price of any pre-recorded CD, album, audiotape or videotape.
- Immediately redeemable-no rebate form to fill out or mail away.
- Simply present check at the register of any participating retailer.

The Raiders first two third-quarter posses-sions produced nothing. But the defense dis-played new life.

On the Broncos second series, tough Raider safety Eddie Anderson stepped in front of a pass John Elway underthrew while pressured by an intense pass rush. On first down from the Denver 40, Schroeder faked inside to halfback Marcus Allen, then passed to fullback Steve Smith in the flat. Smith sped down the sideline and 40 yards equaled seven points. Broncos 24-Raiders 7.

Five plays later, an aroused Raider defense forced a punt. The Broncos Mike Horan boomed a 67-yarder pinning the Raiders on their own nine-yard line. Marcus Allen rushed for nine. Schroeder to wide receive Willie Gault, first for 11 and then for 15. A drive was underway. With second-and-six on Denver's 42, Schroeder found Steve Smith open on the same play-action pass that had worked earlier, but down the other sideline. A downfield block by wide receiver Mervyn Fernandez sealed the out-side running lane as Smith scampered into the end zone untouched. Broncos 24-Raiders 14.

Late in the third period Schroeder hit Fer-nandez for 48 yards, and the fourth quarter commenced with a drive that culminated in a 28-yard field goal by Chris Bhar. Broncos 24-Raiders 17.

On the following kickoff by Bahr, Broncos returner Ken Bell took a big hit by linebacker Reg-gie McKenzie. The ball was loose, and Steve Stra-chan recovered for the Raiders on the Denver 17. Three runs by Allen and an end-around by wide receiver Tim Brown put the ball on the four. Then Allen went inside left for the four and a score Broncos 24-Raider 24, with 9:26 left to play.

The Broncos, behind Elway aerials, retaliat-ed with a long drive that the Raider defense did not stop until Denver reached the eight-yard line. A Rich Karlis 25-yard field goal put the Broncos back on top, 27-24, with just 3:01 showing on the giant scoreboard display.

The Raiders, calm but determined, took over on their own 20, three time outs left plus the two minute warning time out. Schroeder passed to Smith for 16 yards, then to Allen for 11 more. Head coaches change from time to time, but the Raiders full-field, five-receiver passing concepts continued. The constant threat of the vertical passing game helped stretch the Den-

Fullback Steve Smith scores on a pass from Jay Schroeder.

ver defense and open the shorter routes.

With just 35 seconds left, trailing by three, the Raiders faced a crucial fourth-and-four on the Denver 43. Schroeder threw to Allen break-ing outside right for five yards and the first down. Four plays later Chris Bahr kicked a 44-yard field goal—his longest to date in the young 1988 season—to send the game into overtime. Broncos 27-Raiders 27.

The Broncos had the ball three times in the overtime and never crossed midfield against the aroused Raider defense. After their second possession, Denver punted and rookie Tim Brown—the earliest of the Raiders three first-round draft choices that year—electrified the crowd with a brilliant 74 yard return for an apparent game-ending touch-down. The stunned Denver fans quickly went from sorrow to joy when a penalty flag was spotted far upfield and the Raider scoring burst was nullified.

In the next Denver possession, however, John Elway felt the wrath of the Raiders as defensive linemen Bill Pickel, Howie Long and Greg Townsend forced him out of the shotgun, deep toward his right sideline. Elway fired on the run, and safety Zeph Lee fired back—inter-cepting and returning 20 yards to the Denver 31. Smith and Allen alternated carries behind the patched-up offensive line of Rory Graves, Charlie Hannah, John Gesek, Bruce Wilkerson and Steve Wright to position the ball on the Broncos 17. From there, Chris Bahr banged home the field goal from 35 yards on a perfect snap from Trey Junkin and a perfect hold by Jeff Gossett. Final score, after 72 minutes and 35 seconds of energy, effort and emotion, Raiders 30-Broncos 27.

The Raiders were now 26-5-I on Monday Night Football. And the new wearers of the Sil-ver and Black—rookies and veterans alike—had learned a key lesson to build on. So had the ABC-TV crew and millions of television viewers. Names and numbers may change, playing sites may change, but one thing remains constant—RAIDER WILL TO WIN WILL ENDURE FOREVER.

Curt Gowdy, NBC Sports top play-by-play telecaster for many years, called the 1974 AFC Playoff Game between the Oakland Raiders and Miami Dolphins "the greatest game I have ever seen." Gowdy's long time broadcast partner, Al DeRogatis, agreed completely. So did many of the 52,817 present that pre- Christmas Sunday at the Oakland Col-

Don Shula and John Madden would become the only NFL head coaches to win 100 league games in their first ten years on the job. But in this AFC Playoff Game only one of the coaching greats could emerge victorious.

The radio station carrying Raider games in the Bay Area had promoted the game heavily as one during which fans should wear black,

"I've never heard any louder cheering in the Coliseum than when we came out to be introduced," said longtime Raider executive Al LoCasale. "The stadium left the ground."

But the soldout Coliseum went silent in an instant. Miami wide receiver Nate Moore took the short opening kickoff on his own 11-yard line, burst upfield, broke to his left and went untouched into the end zone.

Fifteen seconds off the clock, 89 yards on the field and Miami was ahead, 7-0.

The score stayed that way until the Raiders got the ball for the second time in the second quarter. Quarterback Ken Stabler opened with a nine-yard completion to wide receiver Fred Biletnikoff. Fullback Marv Hubbard slammed inside for five. Stabler then passed over the middle to Hubbard for nine more. Next, halfback Clarence Davis for ten. The big, powerful, machine-like Raider offensive line of Art Shell, Gene Upshaw and Jim Otto—a trio of future Pro Football Hall of Famers—plus George Buehler and John Vella, was taking it to the Dolphins. Three plays later halfback Charlie Smith, a 9.4 sprinter as a collegian, streaked down the middle out of the backfield, pulled clear of the man-to-man coverage by the mismatched Miami linebacker, reached up and pulled in a perfect pass from Stabler to complete a 31-yard touchdown play. Raider 7—Dolphins 7.

Staying primarily on the ground with runners Larry Csonka, Jim Kiick and Benny Malone

In "a sea of hands" Clarence Davis catches a pass for the game-winning touchdown in the final seconds.

iseum. They knew they had witnessed an extra-ordinary event. Forty-million television viewers shared their opinion.

Head Coach Don Shula had led his Miami Dolphins to the last three Super Bowls, winning the last two. In 1974, the Dolphins had gained the AFC East title with an 11-3-0 record, while the Raiders had captured the AFC West crown with a league-best 12-2-0 record. In the previous eight games played between Oakland and Miami since the rivalry began in 1966, the Raiders had a 6-1-1 record. Raider head coach John Madden had a 1-1-0 record against Don Shula's Dolphins.

carry black and wave black. The Coliseum that Sunday was an ocean of black, with kids waving black pennants, socks or towels, local priests waving black cassocks and even a few of the more fervent female fans waving black bras in the breeze.

RAIDER STARTING LINEUPS

Offense			Defense		
WR	21	CLIFF BRANCH	LE	77	BUBBA SMITH
LT	78	ART SHELL	LT	60	OTIS SISTRUNK
LG	63	GENE UPSHAW	RT	80	ART THOMS
C	00	JIM OTTO	RE	82	HORACE JONES
RG	64	GEORGE BUEHLER	LLB	41	PHIL VILLAPIANO
RT	75	JOHN VELLA	MLB	55	DAN CONNERS
TE	88	BOB MOORE	RLB	86	GERALD IRONS
WR	25	FRED BILETNIKOFF	LCB	26	SKIP THOMAS
QB	12	KEN STABLER	RCB	48	NEMIAH WILSON
RB	44	MARV HUBBARD	SS	43	GEORGE ATKINSON
RB	28	CLARENCE DAVIS	FS	32	JACK TATUM

A winning strategy works in any field.

We're proud to be on the Raider team.

As fan signs predicted, Cliff Branch scores on a long bomb from Ken Stabler.

sharing the load, Miami came right back to post three points on a 33-yard field goal by Garo Yepremian with 1:01 remaining in the half, to give the visiting Dolphins a 10-7 lead at the game's midpoint.

Oakland began another march with 11:43 to go in the third quarter, with Stabler to Biletnikoff from 40 yards out. A marvelous leaping catch along the right sideline at the goal line, but the official on the scene signaled, "no good, out of bounds." The undaunted Raiders then moved in again. From the 13, Stabler again went wide right to Biletnikoff. Miami cornerback Tim Foley was draped all over Biletnikoff, but Fred reached up with one hand, fought off Foley, pulled the ball in while staying in bounds to complete a brilliant touchdown play. Raider 14–Dolphins 10.

A 29-yard pass interference call triggered Miami's return march. The Dolphins moved ahead when their superb wide receiver, Paul Warfield, beat the coverage, going into the left corner for 16 yards and a touchdown. But big defensive end Bubba Smith blocked the extra-point attempt. Dolphins 16–Raiders 14.

At the start of the fourth quarter Miami again moved into Oakland territory. Slowed by tough Raider defense, the Dolphins had to settle for a 46-yard field goal, upping their lead to five, 19-14.

With 4:54 left in the game, the Raiders took possession on their own 17-yard line. Stabler went right side to Biletnikoff for 11. Then came the big strike—a trademark of the famed and feared Oakland Raiders vertical passing game. Stabler passed to Cliff Branch on the Miami 27. Branch went to the ground to make the catch, but untouched by Dolphin defenders. Cliff popped right up and ran away from the startled defensive backs to complete a 72-yard scoring play. Raiders 21–Dolphins 19, with 4:37 to go. The explosive Raiders had gone 83 yards in just 17 seconds.

Quarterback Bob Griese brought Miami back immediately, as the fans in the Oakland Coliseum went bananas. With 2:08 remaining to play, Benny Malone swept right end, got free outside,

ducked under a couple of tackle attempts along the sideline and bounded 23 yards to give Miami the lead again, 26-21.

Ron Smith brought the short kickoff back 20 yards, to the Oakland 32. Ken Stabler went to the sideline during the two-minute warning timeout to review strategy and options with head coach John Madden. The Raiders, trailing by five, needed a touchdown. They had 68 yards to travel, two minutes on the clock to make the trip and all three time outs left.

On first down Stabler went to tight end Bob Moore for six yards. Plenty of time left—no reason to force the ball deep as yet. After a short run, Stabler went back to Biletnikoff on consecutive plays for 18 yards along the right sideline and 20 yards down the middle. With one minute left is play, Stabler hit Branch on a quick out to the right for four yards. Then reserve wide receiver Frank Pitts picked up the first down over the middle, bobbling the ball up in the air, but regaining possession before being downed on the Miami 14. Clarence Davis ripped over left guard for six yards. The Raiders then used their final time out.

On first-and-goal from the eight, Stabler dropped back looking for Biletnikoff. At that moment Fred was tightly bracketed by Dolphin defenders. Miami pass rushers were closing in. Finally, with defensive end Vern Den Herder clinging to his legs, pulling him down, Stabler looped the ball left toward the front of the end zone where running back Clarence Davis was working his way back to give his quarterback a target. In a "sea of hands", Davis outfought a crowd of white-jerseyed defenders to come down with the ball and go to the turf clutching the football to his chest in clear, sole possession. The crowd went wild, completely raving wild. People pounded on their Coliseum neighbors. Couples kissed for the first time in years.

It was a scene that Hollywood film producers would reject as "too far-fetched."

This was pro football at its very best. This was classic Raider football—great players, great coaches, great plays and a great game.

The Raiders now were ahead, 28-26, with

Ken Stabler and Fred Biletnikoff receive congratulations from their Raider teammates.

only 24 seconds left. On Miami's second offensive play after the kickoff, linebacker Phil Villapiano intercepted a last-gasp Bob Griese pass at the Oakland 45. Marv Hubbard ran out the clock on two line smashes to the left, behind Upshaw and Shell. Final score: Oakland Raiders 28—Miami Dolphins 26. The Raiders, in a truly classic comeback, had scored twice in the final four minutes and 37 seconds to move on to another AFC Championship Game.

"This has to be the toughest loss I've ever suffered," said Miami coach Don Shula. "The Raiders are a great credit to professional football," he added. "They needed touchdowns to win, and they got them."

The Miami Dolphins under head coach Don Shula were tough to beat. The Miami Dolphins at home in the Orange Bowl were very tough to beat. And the Miami Dolphins with Dan Marino firing are especially tough to beat.

most ever allowed thru passing by the Raiders since the franchise first fielded a team in 1960. No quarterback in the 374 league games that the Raiders had played from September 11, 1960 through November 25, 1984, had ever

moved his club 470 yards by passing against the Silver and Black. Not Pro Football Hall of Fame members like Roger Staubach, Joe Namath, Lenny Dawson, Fran Tarkenton, Johnny Unitas, Dan Fouts, Terry Bradshaw or other great pro passers.

But, you know what? These 1984 Raiders—defending World Champions of Professional Football—gave up 470 yards passing to Marino and the Dolphins and beat them by 11 points, 45 to 34. This classic shootout saw a total of 48 first downs, 919 yards of offense, 711 yards on pass receptions, 81 passes thrown, 137 yards in penalties, 79 points scored and four scoring plays of over 50 yards each. Plus a heroic goal-line stand, a pair of 100-yard individual pass reception games, a 100-yard rushing game, a 100-yard interception game, quarterback sacks, big hits and all the trimmings of the year's best television game.

As the featured NBC Sports game of the day, kickoff time had been set back to 4 p.m. on a humid, windy 80-degree afternoon in Miami to be the second game of the TV doubleheader on both coasts. The Raiders won the coin toss and chose to receive.

On the very first play, Raider quarterback Marc Wilson opened the game with an eight-yard pass in the flat to halfback Kenny King. Three hours and 43 minutes later Wilson would bring the AFC showcase to a close by kneeling

Wide receiver Dokie Williams gets open deep for a 75-yard touchdown play.

On Sunday afternoon, December 2, 1984, in the muggy confines of the aging Orange Bowl, Dan Marino fired more productively than any quarterback the Raiders had faced in their 25-year history. Marino, then only in his second NFL season, completed 35 of 57 pass attempts that afternoon for 470 yards—the

RAIDER STARTING LINEUPS

Offense				Defense		
WR	21	CLIFF BRANCH		LE	75	HOWIE LONG
LT	79	BRUCE DAVIS		NT	62	REGGIE KINLAW
LG	60	CURT MARSH		RE	77	LYLE ALZADO
C	50	DAVE DALBY		LLB	91	BRAD VAN PELT
RG	65	MICKEY MARVIN		ILB	55	MATT MILLEN
RT	70	HENRY LAWRENCE		ILB	58	JACK SQUIREK
TE	46	TODD CHRISTENSEN		RLB	53	ROD MARTIN
WR	80	MALCOLM BARNWELL		LCB	37	LESTER HAYES
QB	6	MARC WILSON		RCB	22	MIKE HAYNES
RB	33	KENNY KING		SS	36	MIKE DAVIS
RB	32	MARCUS ALLEN		FS	26	VANN MCELROY

Cornerback Mike Haynes returns a pass interception 97 yards for a Raider touchdown.

on one knee to run out the clock.

After the first punt, the Dolphins took over on their own 35. Dan Marino started a march by completing passes to his talented wide receivers Mark Clayton and Mark Duper. Then, with a third-and-goal from the Raider three, he threw for Duper in the left flat and found Raider corner Mike Haynes there instead. Haynes picked off the low pass at the three, juked once, headed down the right sideline, picked up an escort from safety Mike Davis and sped a Raider-record 97 yards with the interception to put Los Angeles on the scoreboard first, 7-0. Marino came out firing on Miami's next possession. Six completions later he hit Jimmy Cefalo on the left edge of the end zone from four yards out to tie the score. With this touchdown pass, the brilliant former University of Pittsburgh star had set a new NFL record. In only his second pro season, and his first full season as a starter, Marino had now thrown his 37th touchdown pass in one season—and still had over 47 minutes to play in this game plus two more left on his 1984 league schedule.

A 47-yard strike from Marc Wilson to wide receiver Dokie Williams quickly propelled the Raiders goalward. But then a fumble brought an even quicker end to the drive as the first quarter ended.

In the second quarter, an interception return gave Miami the ball on the Raiders six, and a six-yard burst by Tony Nathan put Miami ahead by six as big defensive end Sean Jones blocked

the extra-point kick. The scoreboard now read: Dolphins 13-Raiders 7.

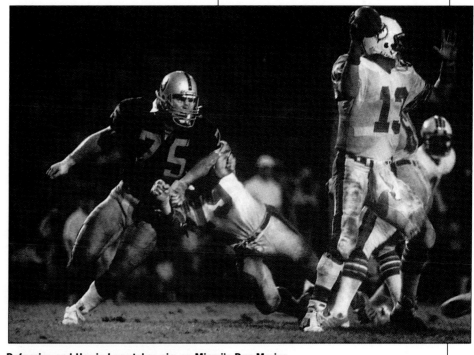

Defensive end Howie Long takes aim on Miami's Dan Marino.

A 42-yard kickoff return by Cle Montgomery started the Raiders back in business. Marc Wilson rolled right and hit wide receiver Malcolm Barnwell along that sideline for 19 yards. Marcus Allen swept left for 15. Then Wilson passed to Allen for 10 down to the Miami 11-yard line. Allen then popped thru between blocks by right guard Mickey Marvin and right tackle Henry Lawrence to put the Raiders back on top, 14-13.

Later in the second quarter, the Raiders pulled ahead, 17-14 on a Chris Bahr 44-yard field goal. The Dolphins then began a march downfield with three minutes left in the half. A pass interference penalty kept the drive alive. A sudden rainstorm then struck, and colorful umbrellas blossomed throughout the Orange Bowl like spring flowers.

Another interference call put Miami on the Raider one-yard line with 45 seconds to play. Big Pete Johnson pounded over left guard on the first-and-goal, but Lyle Alzado stopped him dead in his tracks. Next, Johnson went right and a group of Raider defenders, led by cornerback Lester Hayes, rose up and stopped him just inside the one. Finally, with nine seconds left,

Miami coach Don Shula called his last time out to review his options. Disdaining the field goal, Coach Shula chose to go for the TD and the halftime lead. Woody Bennett powered into the pile behind his left tackle—and went absolutely nowhere. Mike Davis, Howie Long and a wild bunch in Silver and Black said, "no way." As the gun went off, Miami was still one foot from the goal line, and the Raiders were still ahead, 17-13.

But 30 minutes of football, 505 yards of offense and seven touchdowns were still to come!

On the Raiders first second-half possession, a pair of Marc Wilson passes to tight end Todd

right to avoid a rush, fired on the move down the right sideline to a flying Dokie Williams, who went untouched for the score. The Raiders were back on top—for good, finally—31 to 27.

Defensive tackle Bill Pickel got a quarterback sack on the next Miami possession. Cornerback Mike Haynes recorded his second pass interecetion, returning this one 54 yards down the right sideline to the Dolphins 10-yard line. Three plays later, Marcus Allen took a pitchout wide right for six yards and the touchdown. Raiders 38-Dolphins 27.

Miami never quit. Despite defensive pressure from Howie Long, Lyle Alzado, Sean Jones, Reggie Kinlaw, Bill Pickel, Greg Townsend and others who battled heat, humidity and fatigue as well as disciplined pass protectors, Marino threw and threw and threw some more. A nine-yard pass to Duper again cut the Raider lead to just four points, 38-34.

Raider defensive back Odis McKiney recovered the Miami on-sides kickoff attempt on the Los Angeles 44 with 2:09 left on the game clock. After Frank Hawkins gained three inside, the two-minute warning stopped the clock.

When time resumed, Marcus Allen was held to a one-yard gain sweeping right, and Miami took its first time out with 1:52 left. With two time outs remaining, the Dolphins could get the ball back if they stopped the Raiders on the third-and-six at the Los Angeles 48. But these Raiders showed the Dolphins, the sold-out Orange Bowl crowd and the huge national television audience that this night they would not be stopped!

Marcus Allen took the handoff from Marc Wilson, started right, cut back behind tackle Henry Lawrence, leaped over a defender and headed for the goal line. Fifty-two yards later, Allen had his third TD of the game and the Raiders had their tenth win of the 1984 season, enroute to another playoff appearance. Tom Flores was now 5-0 in games against Don Shula.

A tired, weary, but proud band of Raiders had learned firsthand why Dan Marino would one day be a Pro Football Hall of Fame candidate. And a television audience of over 40 million had again learned to respect these Raiders. Home or away, these warriors in Silver and Black continually defied the odds to remain professional sports' winningest team. ◄

Raider quarterback Marc Wilson gets ready to attack.

Christensen and runs by Kenny King and Frank Hawkins put the ball in close. A pass to tight end Dave Casper from seven yards out added seven points. Raiders 24-Dolphins 11.

Just five minutes later, the Dolphins closed the gap to four points again as Marino went deep to Clayton for 64 yards and the score. Amazingly, Clayton fumbled the ball while running all alone in the clear, but the ball bounced right back to him, and he continued in stride for the touchdown.

On their next possession, Miami took the lead—temporarily—when Marino finished an 83-yard march with a 10-yard scoring toss to Clayton along the right sideline. The final quarter would open with Miami ahead 27-24. But head coach Tom Flores and his tough band of Raiders were long on comeback courage though short on time.

With 9:07 left, the Raiders took over on their own 25. One play was all it took to cover the 75 yards ahead. Marc Wilson scrambled to his

Assistant coach Willie Brown and defensive backs Vann McElroy and Mike Haynes celebrate the win.

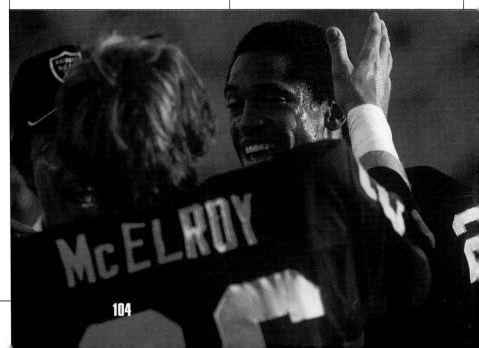

STETSON

EASY TO WEAR, HARD TO RESIST.

The skies were overcast as nearly 60,000 fans streamed into the Oakland-Alameda County Coliseum this mid-October afternoon. The season was as grey as the weather for the Oakland Raiders, now a disappointing 2-4-0 in 1997 going into this game against the undefeated Denver Broncos.

The Raiders were now struggling, though their first two losses had come on the final play of each game and three of their defeats had been by a total of just five points. But making excuses was not part of the four-decade tradition of Raider greatness. It was time to take a stand against the top team in the National Football League. It was time for the proud wearers of the famed Silver and Black to put up or shut up!

Both team were reasonably healthy, having come off their bye week.

"The time helped me," said Raider quarterback Jeff George, the AFC's top-rated passer. "I didn't throw any balls at all while we were off. My arm was a little sore, so the bye couldn't have come at a better time for me."

As it turned out passing would be a secondary weapon in the Raiders offensive arsenal this Sunday. Right from the go, the ground attack would be the key to any success the Raiders would have against the Broncos in this 74th league battle between these two AFL originals. The Raiders dominated the series with a 48-23-2 record since the rivalry began in 1960. But Denver had won the last four games against the Silver and Black, though three were decided by only five points or less.

With four first-year Raiders in the starting lineup—rookie defensive lineman Darrell Russell, safety Eric Turner, guard Lester Holmes and quarterback Jeff George—and three players in their first season as fulltime starters - linebacker Mike Morton, safety James Trapp and running back Napoleon Kaufman—this was certainly not the same team

Denver had downed in '95 and '96.

The Raiders opened the action in high gear as another newcomer—Super Bowl XXXI MVP Desmond Howard—returned the kickoff to the Oakland 29-yard line. On the very first play from scrimmage, Napoleon Kaufman took a delayed hand-off from Jeff George, followed guard Steve Wisniewski and fullback Derrick Fenner up the middle, burst free, broke to the right sideline and went 57 yards before being pushed out of bounds. Then, on third-and-10 from the Denver 14, Jeff George dropped straight back and hit wide receiver James Jett for the game's first score.

"It was a post pattern," recalls Jett. "The defender had pretty good coverage, but Jeff made a perfect throw and I had the right angle to make the catch."

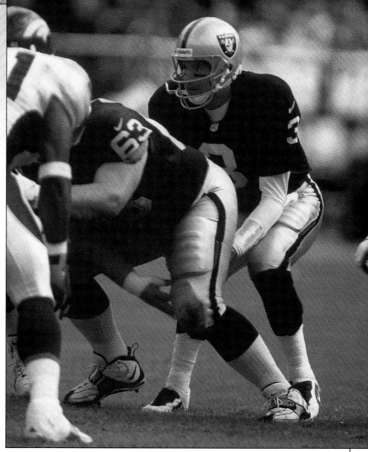

Quarterback Jeff George guided the Raiders against Denver.

Cole Ford added the point-after and the Raiders led 7-0. A sack of John Elway by Chester McGlockton short-circuited one Denver possession but late in the first quarter the Broncos drove 71 yards on eight plays to even the score, 7-7.

RAIDER STARTING LINEUPS

Offense				Defense		
WR	82	JAMES JETT		LE	96	DARRELL RUSSELL
LT	77	PAT HARLOW		LT	67	RUSSELL MARYLAND
LG	76	STEVE WISNIEWSKI		RT	91	CHESTER McGLOCKTON
C	63	BARRET ROBBINS		RE	94	ANTHONY SMITH
RG	71	LESTER HOLMES		OLB	53	ROB FREDRICKSON
RT	72	LINCOLN KENNEDY		MLB	54	GREG BIEKERT
TE	83	RICKEY DUDLEY		OLB	50	MIKE MORTON
WR	81	TIM BROWN		LCB	36	TERRY McDANIEL
QB	3	JEFF GEORGE		RCB	29	ALBERT LEWIS
RB	34	DERRICK FENNER		SS	37	JAMES TRAPP
RB	26	NAPOLEON KAUFMAN		FS	42	ERIC TURNER

Oakland began the second quarter as they had the first, driving 78 yards for a score. Jeff George passed for 45 of those yards, completing the march by drilling tight end Rickey Dudley for five yards and a touchdown to put the hometown Raiders ahead, 14-7.

After his touchdown toss, George jumped into the end zone stands, joining the jubilant fans. "It's nice to have fans like that," the Raider quarterback commented. "In my eight-year career, I've never had fans like that. I ran over and let them know I appreciated them. You see guys painted up, you just want to be with them."

In the final moments of the half, Elway led his team downfield in a war against the clock—and the Raiders. The defense stiffened, and Denver was forced to settle for a field goal to leave Oakland ahead at halftime,

Halfback Napoleon Kaufman breaks loose for 57 yards on the Raiders first play.

14-10. In the opening thirty minutes the battle between running backs Napoleon Kaufman and Terrell Davis of the Broncos had Kaufman ahead in rushing yards, 117 to 42. Jeff George had thrown only nine passes versus 18 tosses by Elway, but two of George's aerials had been for touchdowns.

The Broncos came out firing in the third quarter and drove 80 yards to go ahead 17-14, with the score coming on a three-yard sweep by Terrell Davis.

Denver took over again with 6:11 left to play in the third quarter. Seven plays later, the Broncos faced a third-and-nine at the Oakland 33. Elway set to pass, was pressured, scrambled inside right with defensive end Lance Johnstone in close pursuit.

"At first I thought I was going to sack him, but he got away," said Johnstone. "So I stuck a hand out, grabbed his arm and he coughed it up."

The ball bounced off Elway's leg. As the QB

Linebacker Greg Biekert sacks Denver quarterback John Elway.

tried to recover, he was grabbed by Chester McGlockton, who also batted the ball away. At that point safety Eric Turner scooped up the ball on the Oakland 35 and sped down the left sideline, roaring by the Raider bench. With a burst of speed that displayed his Olympic gold medal form, safety James Trapp got in front of Turner and sealed off the final Denver defender as Turner completed his 65-yard burst to put the Raiders back on top, 21-17.

"That play was huge because we had them out," Elway said after the game. "We were really moving the ball. It was a killer. Everybody in the stadium was quiet, and it just woke everyone up."

A four-point lead with more than 17 minutes left to play was not enough to feel safe in an AFC Western Division game. Especially against John Elway, who had engineered so many late comeback victories in his 15 seasons as field leader of the Broncos.

But when the Raiders next got the ball, an early fourth-quarter fumble gave the Broncos possession on the Oakland 36. After an offsides penalty took it to the 31, the Silver and Black

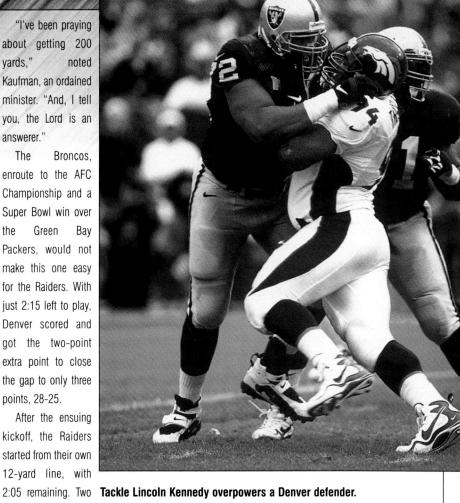
defense rose to the challenge, limiting Denver to just six yards on three plays. A missed 43-yard field goal left the Raiders in front, 21-17.

A 51-yard Denver punt pinned the Raiders on their own eight. Kaufman earned some room on a nine-yard blast off left tackle out to the Oakland 17. Then, on a third-and-one situation, Kaufman burst thru right tackle and raced 83 yards for the score, putting his Raiders on top 28-17. The Raiders had two fullbacks in on the short yardage down—Derrick Fenner and rookie Chad Levitt. Both led Kaufman to the right as tackle Lincoln Kennedy and guard Lester Holmes blew open the hole at the line of scrimmage. Kaufman was hit early, kept his balance, broke free and took off, untouched the rest of the way.

"Napoleon makes these ordinary runs look spectacular," commented perennial Pro Bowl guard Steve Wisnewski. "It looks like up the middle and a cloud of dust, but he breaks them. It looks like two, three or four yards, and he's hitting it for 40 or 50 yards. He reminds me very much of blocking for Bo Jackson."

Napoleon Kaufman's performance this day reminded the record keepers of Bo Jackson also. Kaufman's rushing total of 227 yards broke the previous Raider record of 221 yards rushing set by Bo Jackson on November 30, 1987 in Seattle in a 37-14 Monday night win over the Seahawks.

"I've been praying about getting 200 yards," noted Kaufman, an ordained minister. "And, I tell you, the Lord is an answerer."

The Broncos, enroute to the AFC Championship and a Super Bowl win over the Green Bay Packers, would not make this one easy for the Raiders. With just 2:15 left to play, Denver scored and got the two-point extra point to close the gap to only three points, 28-25.

After the ensuing kickoff, the Raiders started from their own 12-yard line, with 2:05 remaining. Two runs gained nothing, and Oakland was faced with a third-and-ten on their own 12 with 47 seconds left to play. Failure to get the first down here could give Elway the field position to start a final drive for the field goal to tie or a touchdown to win.

Jeff George play-faked to Kaufman and completed a 15-yard strike down the middle to a diving Tim Brown for the game-clinching first down.

"It was obvious who I was going to," said George later.

Darrell Russell pressures Denver's John Elway.

Tackle Lincoln Kennedy overpowers a Denver defender.

"There's no doubt in my mind. If Timmy had two or three guys on him, I was going to Timmy the whole way. That's just one of those situations, third and long, where you know where your money man is."

The Raider defense had held AFC leading rusher Terrell Davis to 3.7 yards per carry and a total of 85 yards rushing. John Elway had been sacked three times. Leo Araguz had averaged 46.4 yards per punt for the Raiders. The two teams had combined for 765 yards total offense. Jeff George had thrown only 12 times, completing nine.

Asked when was the last game in which he had thrown just a dozen passes, George replied, "in second grade!"

But this win over the previously undefeated Denver Broncos was not a second-grade performance for these Oakland Raiders. No, indeed. This was a major league triumph.

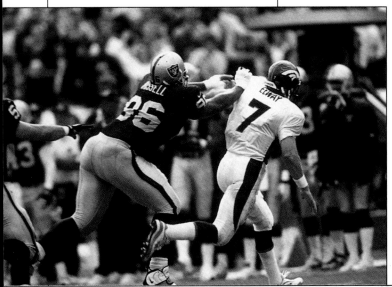

Looking for a flight out...

© 1998
Oakland International Airport

Not a fight getting in?

Then consider Oakland International Airport.

It's so much easier getting to Oakland International than to that other airport across the bay. Upon arrival, you'll find plenty of close-in parking. What you won't find are impossible crowds and long lines.

And factor this. Overall, your trip from your front door to your destination will take a lot less time than if you left from SFO. And will probably cost you a lot less money.

At OAK, the airlines you want to fly are heading for just about anywhere you might want to go. And with so many great fares and convenient ground connections, Oakland International is truly the Bay Area's *value* airport.

So fly OAK and you'll really have something to crow about...

Oakland International
The airport that gives you a flying start.

visit our website at www.oaklandairport.com

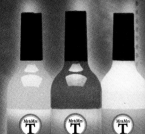
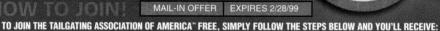

CROWNING GLORIES—
THE SUPER BOWL TRIUMPHS

During the four decades in which the Super Bowl has become the biggest annual one day sporting event in the world, only one team has had a chance to play in the big game in each of those four decades—THE OAKLAND RAIDERS. The Raiders are the only NFL team to have played in Super Bowls in the '60s, the '70s and the '80s, with the '90s still beckoning. Only one other team—the Washington Redskins—has been in this World Championship Game in three decades, but they missed out in the 1960s.

To date, the Silver and Black has won three World Championships of Professional Football—Super Bowl XVIII, following the 1983 season; Super Bowl XV following the 1980 season; and Super Bowl XI following the 1976 season, after losing in the second such World Championship Game, played after the 1967 season.

In these four Super Bowl appearances, the Raiders have scored 121 points while yielding only 66. In their three victories, the Raiders have outscored their NFC rivals by a combined total of 107 to 33. And in the vital first halfs—when the three monumental victories were all but wrapped up—the Raiders totally buried their National Conference opponents by a combined 51 to 6 count.

Though underdogs in all three of their Super Bowl wins—each by the way, played in the hostile climate of an NFC team city—the Raiders rewrote the record book for this pro football championship. The record for the longest run in Super Bowl history belongs to the Oakland Raiders—74 yards by Marcus Allen in the Super Bowl XVIII rout of the Washington Redskins in Tampa Stadium. The Super Bowl record for the longest interception return is still held by cornerback Willie Brown—75 yards in Super Bowl XI in the Rose Bowl in Pasadena. The Raiders in the Super Bowl XV win over the Philadelphia Eagles in the Louisiana Superdome established a record by giving up no quarterback sacks. And in both Super Bowls XI and XV, the Raiders set a record for mistake-free play on offense by not turning the ball over at all in either game. And, in his wins in Super Bowls XV and XVIII, Jim Plunkett set a record for not being intercepted even once.

Though challenged throughout each season by having to win in the super-tough, super-competitive AFC Western Division, the Raiders have still been at their best in their Super Bowl triumphs. In these three wins combined, for instance, Raider quarterbacks never threw a pass interception while completing 41 of 65 attempts for 618 yards, five touchdowns and a 63.1 percent completion rate. And these were not "dink-and-dunk" passing attacks. No, indeed! In these three victories, Raider quarterbacks averaged 9.5 yards per pass attempt and 15.1 yards per reception. Raider quarterbacks, running backs, receivers, return men and interceptors carried the ball 164 times with only one fumble lost.

The Silver and Black averaged 205 yards rushing in their three impressive Super Bowl wins while allowing their opponents to average only 80 yards on the ground. In fact, none of the Raiders NFC opponents could reach the 100-yards mark rushing in these three Super Bowls.

The Raiders—who never trailed in any of their three Super Bowl wins—dominated by using the same demanding organizational philosophy that has carried them to the most lofty pinnacle in professional sports—a total, unyielding commitment to excellence. The Raiders won Super Bowls under different head coaches, different quarterbacks, different running stars, different defenders and specialists and with three different Super Bowl Most Valuable Players. They won Super Bowls indoors or outdoors, on grass or artificial turf, in white jerseys or black jerseys, in different time zones, but with continuity of football philosophy—the varied, multidimensional vertical passing game; the powerful but still explosive running game; an attacking, aggressive defensive in both design and execution; and tough, tenacious special teams.

The Raiders are one of only two teams to have won a Super Bowl as a "wild card" team. The Raiders are the only AFC team to have won more than one Super Bowl since 1979. The Raiders remain the only original American Football League team to have won more than one Super Bowl since 1969—and they've done so three times in that period.

The Raiders have had the greatest players, the greatest coaches, the greatest plays and been involved in the greatest games in the annals of professional sports. The dominating wins in Super Bowl XI, Super Bowl XV and Super Bowl XVIII have indeed been "Crowning Glories" for Raider Decades of Destiny. ◆

The 1976 Oakland Raiders had thundered into the Super Bowl with a 13-1-0 regular-season record and a 2-0-0 mark in the playoffs. These AFC Champions would enter the Rose Bowl on Sunday afternoon, January 9, 1977, having won 12 games in a row. One more win would earn their first World Championship of Professional Football.

The NFC Champion Minnesota Vikings, entering the Super Bowl in search of a first World Championship in four tries, had finished their league campaign with an 11-2-1 record, then had won a pair of playoff games to make it to the finals. The favored Vikings had many vet-

Willie Brown and guard Gene Upshaw, plus linebacker Ted Hendricks who had been in an earlier Super Bowl with the Baltimore Colts.

Raider Owner-Managing General Partner Al Davis had crafted his team with meticulous care. Along with Davis, five of these Raider starters would later be enshrined in the Pro Football Hall of Fame—Biletnikoff, Brown, Hendricks, Upshaw and offensive tackle Art Shell. Others—including punter Ray Guy and head coach John Madden—would be finalists for this prestigious honor.

The two practice weeks leading to Super Bowl Sunday had gone extremely well for the Raiders. Physically and mentally this Raider squad would be perfectly prepared to win. In fact, on the Wednesday before the game, riding back from the final "defensive day" practice of the season, Raider executive assistant Al LoCasale told coach Madden, "Unless our team bus turns over going up the

Quarterback Ken Stabler sets to fire behind the block of tackle John Vella.

canyon to the Rose Bowl Sunday, this one won't even be close."

This belief was rampant among the Raiders. As linebacker Phil Villapiano stated, "We knew by Wednesday we were going to win. The only hard part from then on was waiting for the game." This was a supremely confident football organization with a total commitment to excellence motivating each and every talented wearer of Silver and Black. To this group coming to the

A block by halfback Clarence Davis springs Mark van Eeghen.

erans of previous Super Bowls on every unit. The Raiders had just four veterans who had played for the Silver and Black in Super Bowl II—running back Pete Banaszak, wide receiver Fred Biletnikoff, cornerback

RAIDER STARTING LINEUPS

Offense				Defense		
WR	21	CLIFF BRANCH		LE	72	JOHN MATUSZAK
LT	78	ART SHELL		MG	74	DAVE ROWE
LG	63	GENE UPSHAW		RE	60	OTIS SISTRUNK
C	50	DAVE DALBY		LLB	41	PHIL VILLAPIANO
RG	64	GEORGE BUEHLER		ILB	58	MONTE JOHNSON
RT	75	JOHN VELLA		ILB	39	WILLIE HALL
TE	87	DAVE CASPER		RLB	83	TED HENDRICKS
WR	25	FRED BILETNIKOFF		LCB	26	SKIP THOMAS
QB	12	KEN STABLER		RCB	24	WILLIE BROWN
RB	30	MARK VAN EEGHEN		SS	43	GEORGE ATKINSON
RB	28	CLARENCE DAVIS		FS	32	JACK TATUM

Super Bowl wasn't enough, not nearly enough. These Raiders traveled south from Oakland to headquarter in Newport Beach, train at Irvine and play at Pasadena's Rose Bowl for just one reason—to win the World Championship.

Game day was clear and sunny, with the temperature near 60 degrees at kickoff, a slight breeze out of the northwest and every one of the 103,424 tickets in eager hands. The Raiders were in white jerseys, the Vikings in purple.

Raider special teams captain, tight end Warren Bankston, won the coin toss, and John Madden chose to receive. A 23-yard kickoff return by Carl Garrett and a 25-yard pass from Ken Stabler to tight end Dave Casper put the Raiders in scoring position early. But Errol Mann's 29-yard field-goal try misfired, hitting the left upright and bouncing back.

Ken Stabler smiled after the missed field goal and told coach Madden on the sideline—"No worries, John. There's plenty more points out there for us."

Safety George Atkinson, pound-for-pound the toughest safety in football, broke up a Fran Tarkenton pass intended for Chuck Foreman to doom the Vikings first series. A booming Ray Guy punt of 51 yards after the next Raiders possession pinned Minnesota deep. On third down Tarkenton went long for wide receiver Sammie

White, who could find no free space with Willie Brown in perfect tight man-to-man coverage.

But on the next Raider series, danger threatened. On fourth down from the Oakland 34, Ray Guy had his first-ever NFL punt blocked. It was now Minnesota's ball, first-and-goal on the Oakland three-yard line. But no panic for the Raiders. Just dig in and stop 'em. Play defense. Play tough defense. Play Raiders defense.

On first down, giant rookie defensive tackle Charles Philyaw stopped Chuck Foreman abruptly after one yard. Then, on second down, a wall in white jerseys rose up and stopped Brent McClanahan dead in his tracks. A hit by Phil Villapiano jarred the ball loose, and inside linebacker Willie Hall dove to claim the ball. Raiders' ball on their own three. But not for long.

The Raiders came up on third-and-seven from their six. The play called was "17 Bob Trey O," with Clarence Davis going off left tackle behind a lead block by fullback Mark van Eeghen. Tight end Dave Casper blocked down from his spot on the left side. Guards Gene Upshaw and George Buehler pulled behind the line to get in front of "C.D." as he turned up into the hole, broke to the left sideline and sped for 35 yards. The Raiders were on their way to a Super Bowl record

Linebacker Phil Villapiano signals supremacy by the Oakland Raiders.

266 yards rushing. Clarence Davis would be the leading rusher with 137 yards and "17 Bob Trey O" would be the featured play.

Stabler mixed passes and runs artfully as the Raiders moved to the Vikings seven. There, with

Big tight end Dave Casper powers thru the Vikings secondary.

David Humm holding, Errol Mann drilled a 24-yard field goal down the middle to give the Raiders a 3-0 lead, a lead they would never relinquish this Super Bowl Sunday.

Raider defense was dominating. Three downs and out for the Vikings. Raider ball on their own 36. Stabler opened with a quick out to Cliff Branch for eight yards, then another to Branch for two yards, then 19 yards to Dave Casper. Carl Garrett, in at halfback, cut back inside left end and danced his way for 13 yards. Finally, with third and three on the Minnesota six, Stabler straight back to pass. Fred Biletnikoff split to the right, went downfield, with Viking cornerback Nate Wright in tight coverage. Biletnikoff looked inside, broke sharply to the sideline, caught the perfect pitch from Stabler and was pushed out on the one-foot line.

In 1976, the Vikings were the NFL's toughest team to score on from in close. John Madden

SUPER BOWL XI

capitalized on Minnesota's aggressiveness by calling a beautifully designed play-action pass on first down. Stabler faked inside, then threw to tight end Dave Casper all alone going left through the end zone. Casper went tall for the high-thrown ball, and the Raiders went ahead 10-0 after 7:50 of the second quarter.

Again, Raider might and muscle gave the Vikings absolutely nowhere to go offensively. Cornerbacks Skip Thomas and Willie Brown totally denied Minnesota wide receivers any opportunity to get open. Again, three downs and out. This time a Super Bowl-record 25-yard punt return by Neal Colzie put Oakland just 35 yards away from another score. Four plays into the drive Stabler went to Biletnikoff, again split wide right. This time Biletnikoff faked outside, broke into the post and went sliding to the ground to catch to low pass less than a yard from the Minnesota goal line. Pete Banaszak then bulled his way over right tackle for the touchdown. Mann

missed the extra point, but the Raiders lead climbed to 16-0, the score as the first half ended. Raider defense had limited the Vikings to just four first downs. Raider offense had outgained the Vikings by more than 200 yards, 288 to 86.

There was no let up for Raider defense as the second half opened. The Vikings could not cross midfield on their first two series. Big John Matuszak stuffed Chuck Foreman for

Offensive captain Gene Upshaw leaves no doubt about the Raiders' success.

no gain on a third-and-one, forcing Minnesota to punt. Colzie's 12-yard return brought Ken Stabler and the Raider offense on the field on their own 46. Van Eeghen at right tackle for seven. Davis at left tackle for 16. Stabler to Branch for 10. Then Errol Mann kicks a 40-yard field goal. Raiders 19-Vikings 0.

On the next series, a roughing the punter penalty gave Minnesota a life that a defensive holding call on a long-yardage situation kept alive. Tarkenton took advantage of his breaks and finally got the Vikings on the board with an eight-yard pass to Sammy White to cut the Raider margin to 12 points at 19- 7. The third quarter ended that way.

Five minutes into the final period, a blitzing Ted Hendricks forced Tarkenton to scramble. Tarkenton threw wildly across the field. Line-

Defensive end Otis Sistrunk separates Vikings QB Fran Tarkenton from the football.

Victorious Raiders head coach John Madden and owner Al Davis receive the Vince Lombardi World Championship trophy from NFL Commissioner Pete Rozelle.

backer Willie Hall smoothly cut in front of the intended receiver, intercepted and returned 16 yards to the Raider 46. On third-and-six from midfield, Stabler dropped back, looked the coverage off deep, then hit Biletnikoff breaking open late in the vacant short middle area. Biletnikoff legged it all the way to the Minnesota two, setting up a Raider touchdown for the third time in Super Bowl XI. On the very next play, Pete Banaszak slashed off right tackle, and the Raiders leaped ahead 26-7. The competitive aspects of this Championship Game were now history.

The Vikings kept firing, and the Raiders replied in their aggressive, attacking style. Tarkenton, with the ball on the Oakland 28, fired a short out to the left sideline. Willie Brown, for two decades the finest cornerback in football, proved again that his instincts and reactions were still at the All-Pro level. "Old Man Willie" cut off the receiver's route, drove to the ball, picked it off and headed down the right sideline, flashing by all the Vikings players and coaches as he sped past their now desolate bench.

Linebacker Ted Hendricks and defensive tackle Charles Philyaw carry head coach John Madden as the game ends.

Seventy-five yards later the Raiders had 32 points, and Willie Brown had a Super Bowl record interception return. Mann missed the PAT. Raiders 32-Vikings 7.

Oakland left tackle Art Shell completely shut out Viking defensive end Jim Marshall—no tackles, no assists, no sacks. Upshaw was awesome. At center Dave Dably totally controlled Vikings middle linebacker Jeff Siemon. On the Raider right side, George Buehler and John Vella were equally dominating.

John Madden cleared the Raider bench to be sure every active player saw game action in the Super Bowl win. The Vikings scored a meaningless touchdown with 25 seconds left in the game. By this time bedlam reigned on the Raider sideline. Defensive giants John Matuszak, Charles Philyaw and others carried Coach Madden off on their shoulders. The roar of the crowd was deafening.

Every proud Raider has his own personal, often highly emotional memory of the finish of Super Bowl XI. Mark van Eeghen remembers "standing on the 50-yard line late in the game, thinking I didn't want to leave the field. I knew that once I left, the glory of our victory would wear off some."

Willie Brown recalls thinking, "How winning this game made up for the other Raiders who came before and didn't have a chance to participate on a winning Super Bowl team. This victory meant not only a lot to me, it meant a lot to the entire Raider organization."

John Madden declared, "Super Bowl XI was ours and 10 years from now or 20 years from now Super Bowl XI will still be ours. I'll never take off the Super Bowl ring. It's something I will always cherish."

Every member of the 1976 Raiders, from Al Davis on down, will always cherish this special January, 1977 day when they proved convincingly that at what they did they were clearly the very best in the world.

June 8, 1977 certainly must rank as one of the greatest moments in Raider history. On that afternoon Oakland Raider managing general partner Al Davis presented head coach John Madden, the players, the assistant coaches, the football staff and the administrative staff with their Super Bowl XI rings, emblematic of winning the World Championship of Professional Football a few months before.

In the eleven years since the World Championship Game was first held after the 1966 season, pitting the NFL champs against the AFL champs, on to 1968 when the name of the game was changed to the Super Bowl, and thru 'til the 1976 season when the AFC Champion Oakland Raiders won Super Bowl XI with a deci-

Managing General Partner Al Davis presents their Super Bowl rings to Raider players, coaches, staff and partners.

sive 32-14 win over the NFC Champion Minnesota Vikings, these World Championship rings had become the most valued pieces of award jewelry in the world of sports.

Future Pro Football Hall of Fame enshrinees like coaches Vince Lombardi, Weeb Eubank,

Pete Banaszak and Warren Bankston check out their new Super Bowl rings.

Don Shula and Chuck Noll; quarterbacks Bart Starr, Joe Namath, Terry Bradshaw, Roger Staubach and Bob Griese; and other great players in and not in the Hall of Fame were already proud possessors of these treasured symbols of being the best in the world.

Shortly after their Super Bowl XI victory, Raider owner Al Davis, head coach John Madden and executive assistant Al LoCasale met to plan the design parameters for the Raiders first World Championship ring.

"We wanted a ring so elegant," said Al Davis, "that if one of our people were appointed U.S. Ambassador to the Court of St. James, he would not have to remove it when he was introduced to the Queen."

"Massive elegance," was the watchword for John Madden. "These are big men, and the ring should be the same."

"We did not want a college ring, with a diamond stuck in the middle," recalls Al LoCasale. "And Al wanted a cross-finger ring, not a round one, so that the inscriptions on the top surface would be easy to read."

A number of jewelry companies, large and small, sought to be considered. All had been told of the general guidelines: white gold, diamonds placed in a black stone setting, and a classic design overall.

Eventually, three major firms submitted a set of sketches, then models of their final design. After careful evaluation, the Raiders chose Lenox Awards of St. Charles, Illinois - one of the world's largest importers of diamonds - to create and produce their Super Bowl rings. Lenox Awards chief designer, Elliot Inberg, had captured all the feelings the Raider trio had enumerated and had done so in a unique, powerful design.

The details for the sides of the ring shank were quickly determined.

"On one shank," explained LoCasale, "we wanted two ideas honoring the organization clearly expressed: winning the Super Bowl and winning the AFC Championship. On the other shank we wanted to honor the individual with his name and number, his area (offense, defense, staff), his position and the Raider emblem."

There are 26 five-point diamonds on the ring face. Ten are in the pave' border and represent the previous ten Super Bowls played. The other 16 form the raised football-shaped crest and represent the Raiders 16 victories in 1976. The single one-carat diamond in the middle of the crest symbolizes winning the big one - the World Championship of Professional Football. ◆

SUPER BOWL XV

Fans, media and everyone else in New Orleans the week of Super Bowl XV were greeted wherever they looked by the motto of the Oakland Raiders organization—"COMMITMENT TO EXCELLENCE." This motto and the accompanying Raider logo were emblazoned on giant billboards along highways and streets, on bus stop benches and on the sides of more than 100 city buses. These all helped get a singular message across in this home of the NFC New Orleans Saints—the AFC Champion Oakland Raiders were in town!

The signs were part of the positive environment Raiders Owner-Managing General Partner Al Davis sought for his athletes. The NFC Champion Philadelphia Eagles had been installed as 3½ point favorites in this World Championship Game. The Eagles had, after all, defeated these Raiders 10-7 in Philadlephia just eight weeks earlier, recording an embarassing eight quarterback sacks as they pounded Jim Plunkett from opening kickoff to game's end.

The underdog role sat well with this Raider team. Having started the 1980 season with a 2-3-0 record, then losing starting quarterback Dan Pastorini with a broken leg; having new starters everywhere on offense, defense and special teams; having been returned to Oakland in late March by a court order after having moved the franchise to Los Angeles at the start of that month; having made it all the way to the Super Bowl as a "wild card" team that had to win playoff and conference championship games on the road—this was a team that had not only survived adversity; this was a team that had learned to thrive on adversity.

"The relocations and legal actions were never allowed to become major distractions to our players and coaches," said Raider head coach Tom Flores. "Al Davis would never let these things be distractions. The main purpose was for us to win. Anything else was secondary, and Al would take care of that in his own time. The team never talked about anything but football—winning football. This is a very courageous bunch of guys. They absolutely refused to believe anything but that they could win."

And win they did!

After the 2-3-0 start, the 1980 Raiders went on to win 12 of their next 14 games to end up

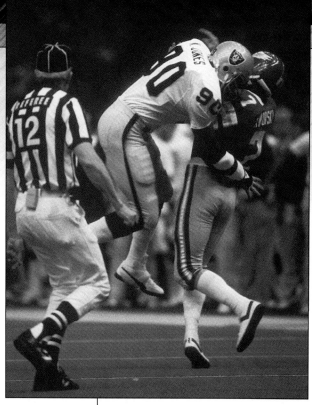

Raider defensive end Willie Jones pounds Eagles quarterback Ron Jaworski.

in New Orleans in January for Super Bowl XV. Included were three postseason wins—27-7 over the Houston Oilers in the wild card game in the Oakland Coliseum, 14-12 over the Browns in Cleveland Stadium and 34-27 in the AFC Championship Game in San Diego.

The Eagles had won the NFC East with a 12-4-0 record, then beat Minnesota 31-16 in the NFC Playoff and the Dallas Cowboys 20-7 in the NFC Championship Game. Under head coach Dick Vermeil they arrived primed and ready to represent their Conference in Super Bowl XV.

But, again as had happened just four years earlier when the Raiders had totally dominated the Minnesota Vikings in Super Bowl XI, this World Championship Game would be a one-sided triumph for the Oakland Raiders.

Quarterback Jim Plunkett, Most Valuable Player in

RAIDER STARTING LINEUPS

Offense				Defense		
WR	21	CLIFF BRANCH		LE	72	JOHN MATUSZAK
LT	78	ART SHELL		MG	62	REGGIE KINLAW
LG	63	GENE UPSHAW		RE	73	DAVE BROWNING
C	50	DAVE DALBY		LLB	83	TED HENDRICKS
RG	65	MICKEY MARVIN		ILB	55	MATT MILLEN
RT	70	HENRY LAWRENCE		ILB	51	BOB NELSON
TE	88	RAYMOND CHESTER		RLB	53	ROD MARTIN
WR	85	BOB CHANDLER		LCB	37	LESTER HAYES
QB	16	JIM PLUNKETT		RCB	35	DWAYNE O'STEEN
RB	30	MARK VAN EEGHEN		SS	36	MIKE DAVIS
RB	33	KENNY KING		FS	44	BURGESS OWENS

this Super Bowl, clearly recalls the Raiders mental approach.

"Al Davis didn't say anything special to us that week about the game, other than the fact that he knew we could win it. It wasn't our job to get caught up in all the legalities. We just had to go out and play Raider football."

These combat-ready warriors in the white jerseys, silver pants and silver and black helmets with the stark pirate logo on each side, quickly established their superiority. On just the third play of the game Raider right side linebacker Rod Martin cut in front of a Ron Jaworski pass on the Eagles 47 and returned it down to the 30.

"The Eagles somehow felt they could exploit Rod Martin," veteran linebacker Ted Hendricks explained. "They decided to attack the right side of our defense, away from me. They tested Rod the whole game, and all they got out of it

Chandler. Chandler was covered, but when Plunkett started forward threatening to run for the score, an Eagles linebacker responded forward leaving a hook spot unguarded that secondary receiver Cliff Branch quickly filled. Plunkett fired, and Branch clutched the game's first score to his chest. Chris Bahr drilled the extra point to put the Silver and Black ahead, 7-0.

Raider defensive game plans were designed to control Eagles top rusher Wilbert Montgomery and force Philadelphia to go to the pass. Design, through practice and intensity, became execution. Montgomery was limited to just 2.8 yards per carry on 16 runs. Jaworski had to go the airborne route and set a Super Bowl record by passing 38 times.

Philadelphia lost one scoring opportunity when a long touchdown pass, Jaworski to wide receiver Rodney Parker, was nullified by an

Quarterback Jim Plunkett earns Super Bowl MVP honors.

about four. The ball is on their own 20. Branch is to the left against Edwards. Chandler to the right against Young.

"Plunkett on a straight drop back. Here comes the rush, steps up, can't find anybody yet, takes off running to the left, throws on the move. It's caught by King at the 40! He'll get down to the 50. He'll go all the way! Nobody there. To the 20. To the 10. To the 5. TOUCHDOWN RAIDERS!"

Running back Kenny King, acquired that year in a trade with the Houston Oilers, had set a Super Bowl record.

"I was running a simple six-yard pattern," said King, "when I saw Plunkett scramble. I took off up the field. The linebacker dropped me when he saw Plunkett scrambling, and Jim got me the ball."

The play covered 80 yards, and the Raiders forged ahead, 14-0.

The Eagles earned only two more first downs in the opening quarter, but using passes to backs and tight ends they were able to move down to the Raiders 13-yard line in an early

Halfback Kenny King finishes an 80-yard scoring play on a pass from Jim Plunkett.

was three interceptions."

It took the eager Raiders offense just a few plays and a few minutes to capitalize on the gift from their alert defense. On third-and-goal from the Philadelphia two-yard line, quarterback Jim Plunkett set up, looking for wide receiver Bob

obvious illegal motion violation. The Eagles subsequently punted, and the Raiders took over deep in their own territory on the 14-yard line. Two downs later Bill King, the long-time voice of Raiders Radio, called the play:

"The Raiders come up third and, oh, just

second-period drive. There defensive tackle Dave Pear and rookie linebacker Matt Millen made big plays, forcing the Eagles to settle for a 30-yard field goal to trail the Raiders, 14-3.

The Raiders missed a long field-goal try midway in the second quarter, and the Eagles got off their best march of the half, going from their own 27 to the Raiders 11. The big Silver and Black defense then rose to the challenge. Three plays later the Eagles were still on the 11. Then Hendricks reached up and swatted a 28-yard field-goal attempt to preserve a 14-3 halftime lead for this Oakland team.

Following the Raider philosophy of pressure football—not percentage football—Flores had his offense firing away right from the start of the third quarter. Plunkett hit Kenny King for 13 along the right sideline, then found Chandler crossing diagonally from right to left for 32 more yards. One play later Plunkett, behind an unbroken wall set up by pass protectors Art Shell, Gene Upshaw, Dave Dalby, Mickey Marvin and Henry Lawrence, went deep down the left side, where

Jubilant Raider players celebrate their World Championship victory.

Cliff Branch outpositioned and outleaped Eagles cornerback Roynell Young for a spectacular touchdown that put the Raiders way out in front, 21-3.

Chris Bahr added a pair of field goals—a 46-yarder in the third quarter and a 35-yarder in the final period. The Eagles finally found the end

zone early in that fourth quarter. Rod Martin got his second and third pass interceptions, defensive end Willie Jones recovered a fumble, safety Burgess Owens was in on nine tackles, safety Mike Davis knocked down three passes. Raider pass protection was near perfect. Mark van Eeghen ran for 80 yards total. Branch caught five passes for 67 yards and two touchdowns, Chandler four for 77 yards and King two for 93 yards and one touchdown. Jim Plunkett completed 13 of 21 for 261 yards and three touchdowns with no interceptions. The Raiders forced four turnovers while commiting absolutely none.

Tom Flores addressed the squad and staff in the crowded Louisiana Superdome locker room after the big win:

"We won the game. We were the best team. We deserve to be the World Champions, and I'm proud of you. I love it. This is the greatest moment of my life. I'm very proud of this bunch of guys."

The final word on this great season by the underdog Raiders belongs to the boss—to Al Davis—as he accepted the Super Bowl trophy from NFL Commissioner Pete Rozelle.

"…You know when you look back on the glory of the Oakland Raiders, this was our finest hour…to Tom Flores, the coaches and the great athletes, you were magnificent out there.

…take pride and be proud. Your commitment to excellence and your will to win will endure forever. You were magnificent!"

Owner Al Davis and head coach Tom Flores receive the Lombardi Trophy after winning Super Bowl XV.

Building a Network Doesn't Get Much Easier!

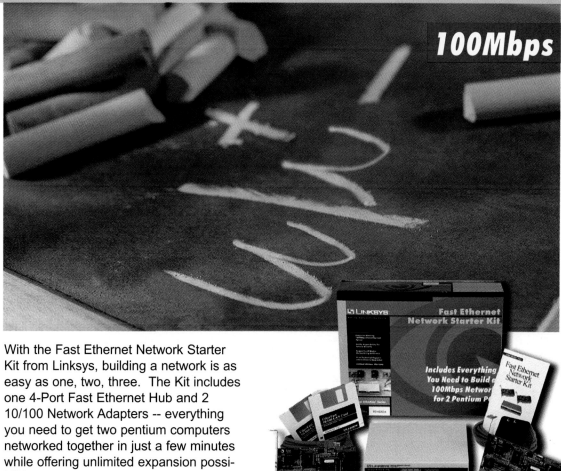

100Mbps

With the Fast Ethernet Network Starter Kit from Linksys, building a network is as easy as one, two, three. The Kit includes one 4-Port Fast Ethernet Hub and 2 10/100 Network Adapters -- everything you need to get two pentium computers networked together in just a few minutes while offering unlimited expansion possibilities.

With a Fast Ethernet Network, you can share files, hard drives, CD-ROMs and printers, exchange e-mail, play networkable games and much more at an incredible speed of 100Mbps.

Simply plug the 10/100 Network Adapters into your computers and connect them to the 4-Port 100BaseTX Fast Ethernet Hub with the included network cable. Building a network doesn't get much easier.

Visit our Web Site at
www.linksys.com
for information on
How to Build
a Fast Ethernet Network

W W W . L I N K S Y S . C O M
1-800-LINKSYS

OfficeMax®

SUPER BOWL XVIII

There is no single day in professional sports to match Super Bowl Sunday. The eyes and ears of the world—not just the sports world—are centered on one stadium, two teams, 90 players.

Only one original American Football League team had won a Super Bowl since 1969—the Raiders in 1976 and again in 1980. Only one team had ever won Super Bowls under more than one head coach—the Raiders under John Madden in 1976 and Tom Flores in 1980.

Tradition is important to the Raider organization, and so a small army of former players were in Tampa, Florida for Super Bowl XVIII as guests of Al Davis and the Raiders: Hall of Fame members George Blanda and Jim Otto were there. So were great Raiders from the sixties and seventies such as Clem Daniels, George Atkinson, Dan Conners, Jack Tatum, Kent McCloughan, Pete Banaszak and more.

Tradition had helped build this 1983 edition of the Silver and Black. But as kickoff time approached, each player and coach in the Raider dressing room beneath the sold-out stands in Tampa Stadium reached inside himself. For a few moments before these black jerseyed warriors took the field, each man was alone, yet in a group bound closely together. Dreams, that for some had started in childhood,

were about to become reality.

The AFL Champion Los Angeles Raiders were in black, the NFC Champion Washington Redskins were in white. Tampa Stadium was ablaze with color—burgundy and gold, silver and black.

This was the big one. This was Super Bowl Sunday, and for all involved there was no

Blocks by the Raider offensive line provides Quarterback Jim Plunkett with great protection.

tomorrow. In America today, being number one is the mark of royalty, and the next three hours would determine who wore the crown in professional football.

The Raiders were the underdogs as they

had been in their two previous Super Bowl wins. The Redskins were the highest scoring team in National Football League history and had beaten the Raiders in Washington earlier in the season, 37-35, in the 1983 season's most exciting game.

But this was a powerful Raider team. Twelve of the 22 Raider starters, plus punter Ray Guy

and kick returner Greg Pruitt, were Pro Bowl selections at least once while with the Raiders. This was a solid, experienced, determined team representing professional sports' winningest organization. Six of these players already owned two Super Bowl rings won as Raiders—Guy, wide receiver Cliff Branch, linebacker Ted Hendricks and offensive linemen Dave Dalby, Henry Lawrence and Steve Sylvester. Seventeen others had earned one Super Bowl ring with earlier Raider World Championship teams.

To get into Super Bowl XVIII, the Redskins had destroyed the Rams, 51-10, in the NFC Playoff Game, then held off the

RAIDER STARTING LINEUPS

Offense			Defense		
WR	21	CLIFF BRANCH	LE	75	HOWIE LONG
LT	79	BRUCE DAVIS	NT	62	REGGIE KINLAW
LG	73	CHARLIE HANNAH	RE	77	LYLE ALZADO
C	50	DAVE DALBY	LLB	83	TED HENDRICKS
RG	65	MICKEY MARVIN	ILB	55	MATT MILLEN
RT	70	HENRY LAWRENCE	ILB	51	BOB NELSON
TE	46	TODD CHRISTENSEN	RLB	53	ROD MARTIN
WR	80	MALCOLM BARNWLL	LCB	37	LESTER HAYES
QB	16	JIM PLUNKETT	RCB	22	MIKE HAYNES
RB	33	KENNY KING	SS	36	MIKE DAVIS
RB	32	MARCUS ALLEN	FS	26	VANN McELROY

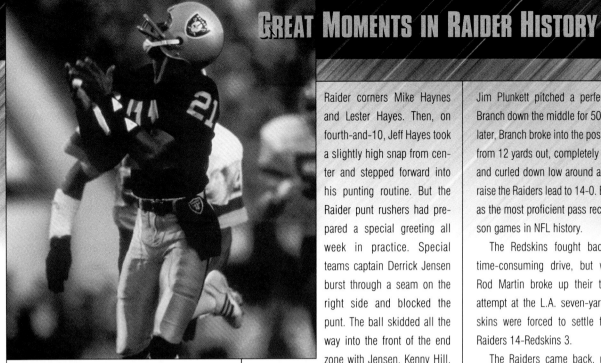

Wide receiver Cliff Branch prepares to complete a 50-yard pass play.

49ers 24-21 to win the NFC Championship. The Raiders had thundered into the Super Bowl after dominating the Pittsburgh Steelers in the AFC Playoff Game, 38-10, and the Seattle Seahawks in the AFC Championship Game, 30-14.

Kickoff came in twilight at 4:45 P.M. Nearly five minutes had elapsed on the game clock when the Redskins were forced to punt from their own 30-yard line. Washington had probed deep on three long passes and found nothing there against

Raider corners Mike Haynes and Lester Hayes. Then, on fourth-and-10, Jeff Hayes took a slightly high snap from center and stepped forward into his punting routine. But the Raider punt rushers had prepared a special greeting all week in practice. Special teams captain Derrick Jensen burst through a seam on the right side and blocked the punt. The ball skidded all the way into the front of the end zone with Jensen, Kenny Hill, Odis McKinney and Lester Hayes in hot pursuit. Jensen got there first, covered the ball, and the Raiders were ahead for keeps, 7-0.

Early in the second quarter, inside linebacker Matt Millen sacked Redskin quarterback Joe Theismann to put Washington in the hole. After the punt, the Raiders started on their own 35 and ended up in touchdown land in just three plays.

Jim Plunkett pitched a perfect strike to Cliff Branch down the middle for 50 yards. Two plays later, Branch broke into the post from left to right from 12 yards out, completely lost his defender and curled down low around a Plunkett pass to raise the Raiders lead to 14-0. Branch continued as the most proficient pass receiver in postseason games in NFL history.

The Redskins fought back with a long, time-consuming drive, but when linebacker Rod Martin broke up their third down pass attempt at the L.A. seven-yard line, the Redskins were forced to settle for a field goal. Raiders 14-Redskins 3.

The Raiders came back, marching to the Washington 39-yard line before a Ray Guy punt pinned the Redskins down at their own 12-yard line.

First-and-ten on their own 12, with only 12 seconds left in the half. But the Raiders remained alert. In the October league game between these teams a screen pass to halfback Joe Washington out of a three wide receiver for-

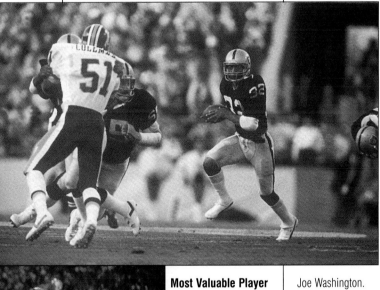

Most Valuable Player Marcus Allen enroute to a record-breaking rushing total.

Cornerback Lester Hayes prepares to go "bump and run" against a Redskin receiver.

mation had triggered a winning rally by the Redskins. When Washington coach Joe Gibbs sent three wides and Joe Washington in, the Raider coaching staff reacted intuitively. Defensive coordinator Charley Sumner countered immediately by inserting speedy linebacker Jack Squirek with specific instructions to go tight man-to-man on Joe Washington.

The three wide receivers went right and Joe Washington went left. A big outside pass rush by defensive end Lyle Alzado forced quarterback Joe Theismann to put extra loft on his soft lob pass toward Joe Washington; over the outstretched hands of the oncoming Alzado. And there was Squirek, grabbing the ball on the move and just hopping into the black-painted

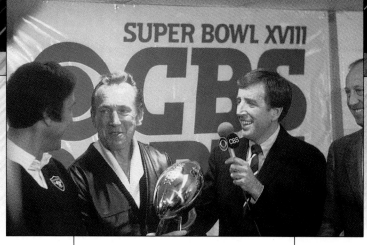

end zone with the football held high in a scoring salute. The interception and touchdown by Squirek put the Raiders ahead at halftime, 21-3, led to a couple of "Holy Toledo's" by radio play-by-play announcer Bill King and set off an explosion of Silver and Black in sold-out Tampa Stadium.

As the second half opened, Washington gallantly fought back, marching 70 yards to score a one-yard plunge by future Hall of Fame inductee John Riggins. Then Raider reserve tight end Don Hasselbeck penetrated sharply, reached high and blocked the extra point as Raider special teams continued to be a key element in the relentless pursuit of glory.

The Raiders now had 21 points, the Redskins 9. But the Redskins would score no more in the nearly 26 minutes that remained to play.

Head coach Tom Flores gathered his Silver

Head Coach Tom Flores and owner Al Davis share the World Championship trophy in the Raider lockerroom.

nerback Darrell Green was flagged for pass interference on a bomb from Plunkett to speedy wide receiver Malcolm Barnwell. Plunkett then went underneath for completions to Branch, tight end Todd Christensen and fullback Frank Hawkins to move goalward relentlessly. Finally, from the Washington five, Marcus Allen skillfully danced free inside and dove into the end zone for the touchdown to put the Raiders ahead by 19 points, 28-9.

With 1:35 left in the third quarter, the Raiders only turnover put the Redskins just 35 yards from the end zone. But on fourth-and-one from the Los Angeles 26, John Riggins powered off left tackle behind the blocking of the highly publicized "Hogs"—the Redskins massive front line. Raider linebacker Rod Martin overpowered the tight end trying to block him, clogging the off-tackle hole and giving Riggins nowhere to go. Safeties Mike Davis and Vann McElroy roared in to support and the Redskins remained one yard short. The Raiders took over on their own 26-yard line.

Marcus Allen took over from there. Allen started left, went too wide for his blocking, found heavy traffic, reversed his field, saw a lane inside, burst free of pursuit, angled left as he sped downfield, picked up an escort from Branch and went 74 yards for a then-record Super Bowl

longest run from scrimmage. The touchdown put the Raiders way out in front, 35-9.

For all practical purposes, Super Bowl XVIII was now history. The Raiders added a 21-yard field goal by Chris Bahr in the final minutes. Coach Flores cleared the bench to allow every proud Raider to see action in this masterful performance. Mike Haynes got an interception, Jeff Barnes and Mike Davis added sacks. The statistics piled up; the smiles grew wider; the roar of the crowd grew louder.

The clock ticked down: five, four, three. Frank Hawkins ran the final sweep and the gun went off. The Raiders 38, the Redskins 9. The Raiders were again the World Champions of Professional Football. The third time in just eight years!

In accepting his third Super Bowl trophy Owner Al Davis appropriately memorialized the team, the organization and the overwhelming triumph.

"Just win, Baby! Two years ago when we first came to Los Angeles, I really believed the greatness of the Raiders would be in the future. With all the great teams we've had, I think today that this organization, this team, this coaching staff dominated so decisively that two things must be said.

"Not only, in my opinion, are you the greatest Raider team of all time, I think you rank with the great teams of all times to have ever played any professional sport."

The joyous Raider lockerroom was still as Al Davis continued:

"Tom Flores isn't just a great coach in our league. With all due respect, he's one of the great coaches of all time.

"I want to say one thing to the fans and great players who wore the Silver and Black in the past all over the country. And I want to pay tribute to my partner, Ed McGah, who died earlier this winter. Again, you were magnificent. You dominated. And I love all of you, and you know that." ◆

Victorious head coach Tom Flores rides to glory on the shoulders of his troops.

and Black-clad warriors on the sideline. "No let up, no let up. Just 30 minutes of Raiders football and its ours," Flores exhorted. And there would be no let up. No way. This game, this season, this league, belonged to the Raiders.

The threat of the feared Raider deep passing attack opened the short routes after Redskin cor-

"Mind doing that again? I was changing my battery." Only Sony Handycam camcorders allow you to record with a 12-hour battery.* And along with this added stamina, you'll also get up-to-the-minute battery life readings. So you'll always know exactly how much recording time you have left. Because no moment is going to repeat itself. No matter how politely you ask.

SONY

www.sony.com/handycam

What do organizations like the Children's Hospital, the Special Olympics, the Boy Scouts of America, the Food Bank, the Boys and Girls Clubs, the California Department of Social Services, the Mother Wright Foundation and the Police Activites League, for instance, have in common? Obviously, these groups and many others support very worthy causes throughout the Bay Area. Not quite so obviously, however, is that these organizations and so many more, receive support in their activities over the years from the Oakland Raider organization, Raider players, Raider coaches and staff, the Raiderettes and the families of these genuinely interested people.

Whether it's Halloween parties, Thanksgiving feedings, Christmas gift giving, hospital visits, school assemblies, fund-raising functions of all kinds, multicultural carnivals, DARE presentations and activities, Toys for Tots drives; whether it's inseason or offseason; whether it's a large group or small, public or private, the Oakland Raiders are out in the community.

The Raider/Boy Scouts of America Golf Tournament, first in Los Angeles and for the last two years in Oakland, has raised $2 million to support Boy Scout activities. The fundraising success of the most recent tournament in June is hopefully just a preview of even bigger and better things to come, as the local corporate community becomes more aware of this great day with Raider players, coaches and former players that more importantly helps fund the most diversified of Boy Scout councils.

Raider players, former players, staff and Raiderettes make hundreds of appearances with youth groups, social clubs, school groups and the like to encourage the development of academic, social, emotional and cultur-

Head Coach Jon Gruden at the 1998 Raiders/Boy Scouts Golf Tournament.

al skills. They visit adult groups to help raise the funds needed for such worthy causes to operate and prosper.

These Raider athletes and other personnel all live in the Bay Area at least six months of the year and year-round for many. This is their community, too. They raise their families here, send their children to schools here, use educational, recreational and health facilites here. This is their home, too.

Athletes—Raiders and others alike—give of their time, their effort, their experience and their funds to help in a myriad of ways. They serve as celebrity waiters, guest speakers, autograph signers, models, golfers, bowlers, baby-sitters, good listeners and hand in hand with Commitment to Excellence in the Oakland Raider organization.

Defensive tackle Russell Maryland receives check he won as Raider Man-of-the-Year to be used for the Russell Maryland Charity Foundation.

Cornerback Albert Lewis leads group in a "Sports in the Classroom" session.

Raiders/Boy Scouts Golf Tournament has raised over two million dollars.

Offensive guard Steve Wisniewski visits patients at Children's Hospital-Oakland.

Wide receiver Tim Brown and wife Sherice filming United Way television spot about "9-1-1 for Kids."

Television of National Football League games has helped showcase one special aspect of the Raider organization—one fabulous part—to millions of football fans locally, regionally, nationally and internationally. This part of the organization has become the standard of excellence—not just in football in general or professional football in particular—but in any phase of sports today.

These standard-setters are the Raiderettes—"Football's Fabulous Females." These are the most glamorous girls of the game, the epitome of class and beauty. These are the lovely ladies who represent the Oakland Raiders at home games, special events and promotions throughout California, the United States and many foreign countries.

The 1998 Raiderettes are an extraordinary group of young women ranging in age from 18 to the mid 30's, from five-foot-one inches tall to a towering six feet, averaging five-foot-six. They were born in 13 different states and five foreign countries (Guam, Guatemala, Japan, Philippines and Russia).

These Raiderettes have occupations ranging from college students to retail clerks, nurses, actresses, dancers, models, sales representatives, aerobics instructors, receptionists, mortgage brokers, flight attendants, accountants, hair stylists, marketers, merchandisers, artists and educators, among others. There is even one welder.

Some of the women in this 39th unit in Raiderette history are married, some

are parents, most are single—and all are talented and beautiful. Hundreds of California's prettiest competed for places on this 1998 squad during a pair of tension-packed weekends in May. Tryouts were organized by long-time Raiderette Director Mary Barnes. Of the original group of candidates, 165 or so made it into the finals and 50 were ultimately selected as Raiderettes by a distinguished

Raiderettes
Football's Fabulous Females®

panel of judges headed for the 25th consecutive year by Raider Executive Assistant Al LoCasale.

Thirty-four of the squad were Raiderettes before, and 16 were newcomers—the class of 1998.

A few years ago the national newspaper, "USA TODAY" conducted an extensive poll of NFL players. When asked to name the best cheerleader unit in the League, these players overwhelmingly chose the Raiderettes. Over 65 percent—nearly two out of every three players

polled—named the Raiderettes as pro football's very best. That came as no great surprise to the in-stadium audience, television viewers and others who have watched the Raiderettes in action or on their annual best-selling calendars and posters, videos or trading cards or have met some of the women during their many charitable or promotional appearances.

The popularity of the Raiderettes throughout the United States and overseas continues to grow—and deservedly so. In recent years, the Raiderettes have performed at NFL American

Bowl Games in London, England; Tokyo, Japan; and Barcelona, Spain. Raiderettes were chosen to organize the cheerleader units for three of the six World League of American Football teams—the Barcelona Dragons, London Monarchs and Scottish Claymores.

Through four decades of performances, hundreds of lovely young women have worn the Silver and Black with pride

and poise, class and distinction, as symbols of the Greatness of the Raiders.

Former Raiderettes have gone on to be doctors, lawyers, media personalities, teachers, corporate leaders, entrepreneurs, show business performers, administrators or executives. Many have helped establish businesses throughout California, Hawaii and the West. Most have built families and become deeply involved in their local communities. Friendships that began among total strangers at Raiderette tryouts and blossomed at line drills and squad rehearsals have continued over the years. Raiderette reunions rival the very best of high school or college class get-togethers. A

few of the Raiderettes have married football players, but many are raising future star student-athletes. Some now coach cheerleader squads at high schools or Pop Warner Football Leagues in their own communities.

There are former Raiderettes serving in restaurant or hotel management, residential or commercial real estate, in law enforcement and as flight attendants. Some even help design or build the aircraft in which others travel to work.

Along with their grace, beauty and dance skills, Raiderettes share a willingness to work, great pride of performance and a joy in entertaining others. They love putting on their distinctive uniforms and turning on the crowd. They truly enjoy what they are doing—despite their very substantial investment of time and effort.

As far as athletics are concerned, the current Raiderette unit contains those who have lettered in gymnastics, track and field, basketball, baseball, softball, volleyball, swimming, diving and even flag football. They have won awards in snow skiing, water skiing, ice skating and roller skating, martial arts, horseback riding, cross-country races, marathons, pageants, beauty contests, dance competitions, motorcycle races and automobile races. Some jog or practice aerobics; others train with weights to maintain their physical excellence. These are health conscious, diet conscious, fashion conscious,

appearance conscious young women who care about how they look, how they act and how they perform. They well realize they are role models to many youngsters and they take these responsibilities seriously.

These Raiderettes are modern women-of-the-now-generation. They are computer literate, electronics educated, well-read, knowledgeable in a wide variety of academic disciplines. A number speak a second language; some already have or are presently pursuing advanced college degrees.

The 1998 Raiderettes—and talented choreographers Karen Kovac and Ramona Braganza—are well aware that they represent one of the premier organizations in sports. They have participated in seminars and lectures on the Raider Tradition of Greatness. They have visited with former Raiderettes to learn of the duties and responsiblities necessary to maintain the character and reputation of those who proudly preceeded them. They have read books, viewed movies and videos to learn some of the history of the Raiders and the Raiderettes. They have learned that quality and enthusiasm and character are as essential as beauty of face and form and that dignity and integrity are as important as dance routines. They have, in all respects, justly earned their famous tagline as "Football's Fabulous Females."

For the past two decades, the Sunday before and the Sunday after Mother's Day have been very memorable dates for thousands of beautiful young California women. These two May Sundays each year have been exciting, fun-filled, pressure-packed and more for a group of lovely ladies from 18 years old on up; a group of all ethnic, cultural, racial and national backgrounds; a group containing the petite, the average-sized and the queen-sized; blondes, redheads, brunettes, short hair, long hair, whatever.

But every girl in these groups has one thing in common—they want to be a Raiderette. They want to be one of "Football's Fabulous Females"—the prestigious cheerleading, pom-pon, dance and public relations squad that represents the Oakland Raiders at home games, promotional and charity events and special activities locally, regionally, nationally and internationally.

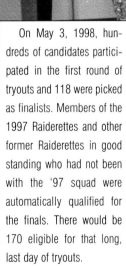

On May 3, 1998, hundreds of candidates participated in the first round of tryouts and 118 were picked as finalists. Members of the 1997 Raiderettes and other former Raiderettes in good standing who had not been with the '97 squad were automatically qualified for the finals. There would be 170 eligible for that long, last day of tryouts.

During the break between the tryouts and the finals, all candidates had two opportunities to learn a short dance routine designed to showcase their coordination, sense of rhythm, agility, balance,
stage presence and ability to learn. The routine—designed by Raiderette choreographer Karen Kovac and taught by Karen and assistant Ramona Braganza—was new so that the former Raiderettes were not any more familiar with it than the new candidates. Some of the girls videotaped the routine to be able to work on it throughout the two-week period. Many formed small groups to work together as they rehearsed. Friendships were already forming that would last for years to come.

On the morning of Sunday, May 17, 1998, the finalists registered, completed required paperwork, were weighed in, then photographed dressed as if attending a party. Raiderette director Mary Barnes supervised and organized the activities, serving as a source of advice and encouragement to all.

Meanwhile, the panel of 18 judges—some veterans of Raiderette tryouts in previous years, others new to the task—were briefed by Raider

FESTINA™

FESTINA. IT'S ABOUT TIME.™

FESTINA, the fastest growing watch line in Europe, has finally arrived in North America. Pictured above Richard Virenque, world class rider for the Festina Racing Team and the new Mecaquartz.™ As the Official Timer of the Tour de France, we understand the importance of a split-second. **FESTINA. It's About Time.™**

executive assistant Al LoCasale, who has been in charge of the selection process since 1974.

The first group of 25 finalists entered at 9:00 a.m. for their individual interviews, still in their party best. After each candidate had an opportunity to talk about herself, her current activities and future plans, the full group of 25 was assembled to provide a final look for the judges. Seven such groups went through the same procedure to complete this phase of the finals. Every interview was videotaped for later review.

Next, again in their groups of 25, the girls returned in dance attire to individually perform the required routine. The judges earlier had seen choreographer Karen Kovac demonstrate it a number of times and knew what the standards were for a satisfactory presentation. Intense coaching for those who made the squad would improve their performance if basic dance skills were present.

Once the dance evaluations—also videotaped—were completed in the early evening hours, the judges assembled to review each candidate and cast their votes. Photographs of the girls taken at the start of the day were used to be sure everyone recalled each finalist. The videotapes were similarly available. Every judge approached their job very seriously with a variety of opinions expressed until consensus was reached. Fifty finalists were named as members of the new 1998 Raiderette squad—the 39th such unit to represent the organization. The quality of the finalists was such that the deci-

sions were difficult.

As one experienced judge commented, "we could have picked another great squad for one of the NFL teams that doesn't presently have cheerleaders."

This annual rite has become a highlight of the spring scene for the Raiders—and hopefully a memorable experience for every candidate, every finalist, and every sucessful Raiderette selected. For information on the 1999 tryouts, prospective candidates should write or call the Raiderette Department, 1220 Harbor Bay Parkway, Alameda, CA 94502 (510/864-5000) AFTER MARCH 1, 1999. Tryouts for the 40th Raiderette squad are tentatively scheduled for May, 1999. ◆

Raiderettes
Football's Fabulous Females ®

AL DAVIS

LIMITED PARTNERS

Ginny Boscacci, Rita Boscacci, John Brooks, Jack Hartman, Ed McGah, Bob Seaman, Doray Vail, Gertrude Winkenbach

COACHING STAFF

Jon Gruden . . . . Head Coach
Dave Adolph . . . . Linebackers
Fred Biletnikoff . . . . Wide Receivers
Chuck Bresnehan . . . . Defensive Backs
Willie Brown . . . . Squad Development
Bill Callahan . . . . Offensive Coordinator, Tight Ends
Frank Gansz, Jr. . . . . Special Teams
Garrett Giemont . . . . Strength and Conditioning
Robert Jenkins . . . . Offensive Assistant
Don Martin . . . . Quality Control - Defense
John Morton . . . . Offensive Assistant
Skip Peete . . . . Running Backs
Keith Rowen . . . . Offensive Line
David Shaw . . . . Quality Control - Offense
Willie Shaw . . . . Defensive Coordinator
Gary Stevens . . . . Quarterbacks
Mike Waufle . . . . Defensive Line

ADMINISTRATIVE STAFF

Amy Trask . . . . Chief Executive
Al LoCasale . . . . Executive Assistant
Jeff Birren . . . . Legal Affairs
Marc Badain . . . . Finance
Tom Blanda . . . . Finance
Morris Bradshaw . . . . Senior Administrator
Valerie Bronger . . . . Legal Affairs
Peter Eiges . . . . Ticket Operations
Susie Elliot . . . . Raider Image
Scott Fink . . . . Business Affairs
John Herrera . . . . Senior Executive
Roxanne Kosarzycki . . . . Legal Affairs
Jennifer Levy . . . . Finance
Marc McKinney . . . . Public Relations Assistant
Jim Otto . . . . Special Projects
Mario Perez . . . . Public Relations Assistant
Derek Person . . . . Finance
Dawn Roberts . . . . Business Affairs
Mike Taylor . . . . Public Relations

Kristi Bailey, Mary Barnes, Trisha Kubota, Claudia Madro, Cheryl Nichols, Jamie Nutile, Karen Otten, Carolyn Paul, Monika Sweetwyne, Lori Ward . . . . Front Office Staff
Ken Irons . . . . Building and Grounds
Mickey Elliot, David Graham, Jerry Soifer . . . . Photographers
Karen Kovac, Ramona Braganza . . . . Raiderette Staff
Tony Salvadore, Rod Brooks, Darren Chan,
Tom Flores, Artie Gigantino, Lee Hammer,
David Humm, Greg Papa, Kevin Radich, Dan Sileo . . . . Raider Radio

FOOTBALL STAFF

Bruce Allen . . . . Senior Assistant
Ken Herock . . . . Personnel Executive
George Karras . . . . Pro Scouting Consultant
Mark Arteaga . . . . Administrative Assistant to Head Coach
Angelo Coia . . . . Player Personnel
Jonathan Jones . . . . Trainer
Bruce Kebric . . . . Player Personnel
Jon Kingdon . . . . Player Personnel
H. Rod Martin . . . . Head Trainer
Mickey Marvin . . . . Player Personnel
Mark Mayer . . . . Strength & Conditioning
David McCloughan . . . . Player Personnel
Kent McCloughan . . . . Player Personnel
Dave Nash . . . . Video Coordinator
Jim Otten . . . . Video Operations
John Otten . . . . Computer Operations
Sheratt Reicher . . . . Player Personnel
Bob Romanski . . . . Equipment Manager
Richard Romanski . . . . Equipment Assistant
Scott Touchet . . . . Assistant Trainer
Bill Urbanik . . . . Player Personnel
Jack Barhite, Butch Enriquez,
Paul Kelly, D.J. McCarthy, ... Football Office Staff
Kevin Bazzy, Keith Hinkley,
George Jones, Al Olks, Woody Wheeler . . . . Equipment Assistants
Dr. Robert Albo . . . . Medical Director
Dr. Stephen Corday, Dr. Warren King, ... Medical Consultants
Dr. Fred Nicola, Dr. Warren Strudwick
Dr. Derric Desmarteau . . . . Dental Consultant

PHOTOGRAPHERS AND ARTISTS REPRESENTED IN THIS BOOK:

Aerial Sport Photography, Inc., Andrew Bernstein, John Biever, David Boss, Greg Cava, Ray Chavez, Sam Cohen, Merv Corning, Scott Cunningham, Frank R. Denevi, Dennis Desprois, Mickey Elliot, Norm Fisher, David Martin Graham, Dan Honda, Fred Kaplan, Ed Lee, Lenox Awards, Inc., Long Brothers Photography, Tak Makita, Al Messerschmidt, Peter Read Miller, Bill Mount, NFL Properties, Jen Oliver, Russ Reed, Roger Sandler, Manny Rubio, Jerry Soifer, St. Petersburg Times, Kevin Terrell, Tony Tomsic, Corky Trewin, James Whitaker, Michael Zagaris, Jim Zar

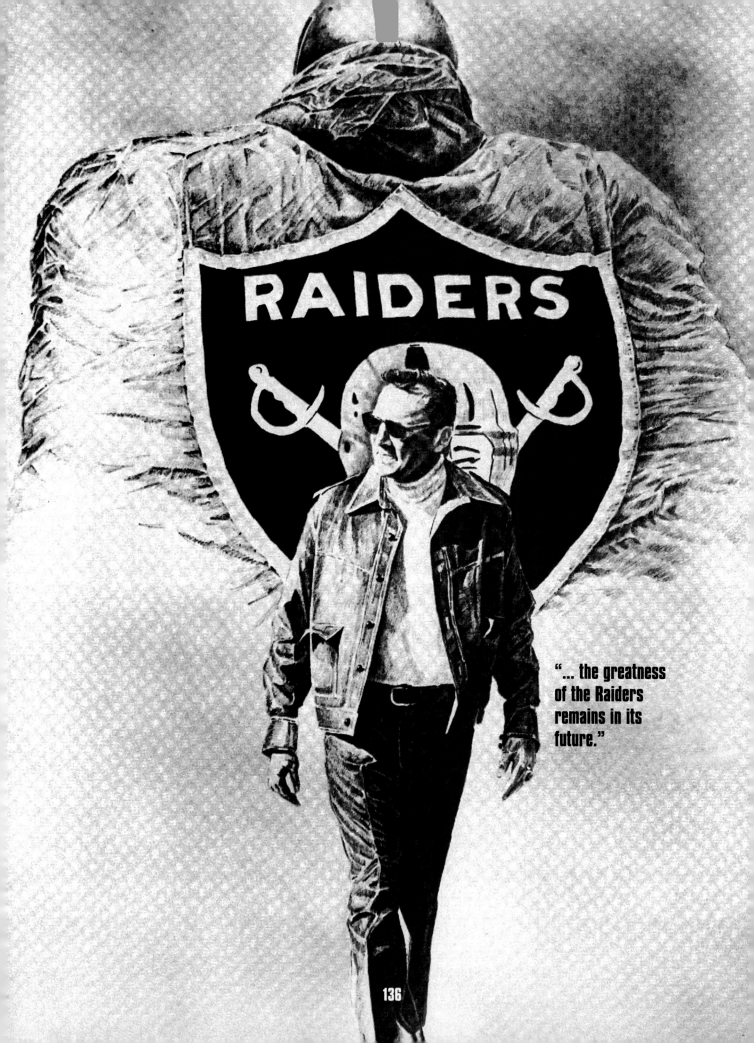

" ... the greatness
of the Raiders
remains in its
future."